Advance Praise

"Being a business owner is tough. Throw in financial management and eyes glass over. Who knew bookkeeping could be such a daunting obstacle? Thankfully, Liz Lajoie's new book, **From Zero to Zen**, walks the small business owner gently through the money side of their business. The book is supportive, practical, and a gift to the many hardworking women making a difference every day!"

– Michael F. Kay, CFP
Author of *The Feel Rich Project*
www.financial-lifefocus.com

"Liz Lajoie breaks down small business finance into easy, manageable bites for anyone who finds numbers intimidating. You'll learn exactly what you need to be doing (and what you don't have to worry about) when it comes to managing your finances – so you can run and grow your business like a pro."

– Jenny Shih
Business Coach and Consultant
www.jennyshih.com

T0163751

"In **From Zero to Zen**, author Liz Lajoie artfully combines financial wisdom with spiritual insight. It's a must-read book that helps heart-based entrepreneurs feel great about knowing their business numbers and finances. She takes something that is often scary and turns it into an act of service. Thank you, Liz!"

– **Tami Stackelhouse**
Founder, International Fibromyalgia Coaching Institute
www.ifcinstitute.com

"Liz is a master at her craft, and **From Zero to Zen** is the perfect distillation of her mastery into an easy to understand, easy to implement plan for those of us who cringe thinking about our finances. This book makes the daunting task of building (or even scarier, repairing) your financial foundation feel like it's not only doable, but like it could be enjoyable. I never thought that was possible before Liz and her book came into my life. Thank you, Liz, for opening my eyes to the Zen hidden within my numbers!"

– **Amy Birks**
The Strategy Ninja
www.amybirks.com

From Zero to Zen

from ZERO to Zen

*Secret Keys to Nurturing Your Numbers
and Finding Financial Flow*

LIZ LAJOIE

NEW YORK

LONDON • NASHVILLE • MELBOURNE • VANCOUVER

From Zero to Zen

Secret Keys to Nurturing Your Numbers and Finding Financial Flow

Published in New York, New York, by Morgan James Publishing in partnership with Difference Press. Morgan James is a trademark of Morgan James, LLC.
www.MorganJamesPublishing.com

The Morgan James Speakers Group can bring authors to your live event. For more information or to book an event visit The Morgan James Speakers Group at www.TheMorganJamesSpeakersGroup.com.

ISBN 9781683507048 paperback
ISBN 9781683507055 eBook
Library of Congress Control Number: 2017912140

Cover Design by:
Rachel Lopez
www.r2cdesign.com

Interior Design by:
Chris Treccani
www.3dogcreative.net

In an effort to support local communities, raise awareness and funds, Morgan James Publishing donates a percentage of all book sales for the life of each book to Habitat for Humanity Peninsula and Greater Williamsburg.

Get involved today! Visit
www.MorganJamesBuilds.com

Table of Contents

Introduction   *xi*

Chapter 1   The Money Mind Trip   1
Chapter 2   My Own Less-Than-Shiny Yellow
             Brick Road   19
Chapter 3   The Journey from Zero to Zen   33
Chapter 4   Happy Clients Equal a Happy You   49
Chapter 5   Show Me the Money!   63
Chapter 6   Pay the Piper   77
Chapter 7   Timing Really Is Everything   93
Chapter 8   One for the Money, Two for the Show   109
Chapter 9   The Best Laid Plans   121
Chapter 10   Finding Your Balance   131

Further Reading   *147*
Acknowledgments   *149*
About the Author   *151*
Thank You   *153*

Introduction

"Financial success becomes a transformational journey, a personal healing, a sacred initiation, empowering you to become all you're meant to be and to do what you're put on this planet to do."

–Barbara Stanny

I have a confession to make. I *hate* doing laundry. We all have those household chores that stare us in the face every week, or month, or year, that we just don't want to do. Clean the bathroom? I'm all over it. Do the dishes? I'm there with a smile on my face. Doing laundry, however, feels like crossing the Alps... long and tortuous. I watch it piling up and I start feeling agitated and irritated, until I can't stand looking at it anymore so I slam the closet door shut. Eventually, when this huge weight of "should" wears me down, I face the mountain of dirty clothes and wash the darn things.

You know how it feels when you have a task like that hanging over your head? Maybe it's not laundry. Maybe it's scrubbing the bathtub or changing the sheets. Usually the task itself isn't particularly hard; it only seems that way because we've got a mental block about it.

You may feel the same way about managing your money. For a lot of people (women in particular), taking care of our bookkeeping is the last thing we want to do. We'll find anything and everything else to do before we crack into our finances. Like tackling my enormous heap of dirty laundry, doing financial work can make us annoyed, cranky, and downright uncomfortable. That's normal when facing a task that doesn't sing to you. There's no right or wrong about it: many of us simply hate dealing with our money.

Here's something else I know, though. Clean clothes make me feel comfortable and let me present myself to my best advantage. I'm a shower-every-day kind of girl and putting on dirty clothes over a clean body feels icky. When I'm wearing clean clothing, I feel more confident, whether I'm dressing for a power meeting or lounging around the house. I feel more like myself. So, while I know that I *hate* doing my laundry, I *love* having clean clothes to wear. That's why I don't let my washing pile up anymore – because I know if I do it I'll feel better in the long run. In reality, doing the laundry doesn't take that much time and, once I actually get started, it's a snap. Do I still feel that crushing "I don't wanna!" in the minutes before I start collecting my clothes and getting out the detergent? Absolutely. But I power through because I can see the soft white sheets and feel the "ready to take on the world" tactile reaction I have to a newly laundered shirt. The outcome makes the drudgery worthwhile.

Having clean books in your business works the same way. And it can be as simple as learning to do laundry. I promise. If you've mastered doing laundry, you can master this task, with much greater potential for results and reward. How? By acknowledging your discomfort around money, setting up good systems that are actually easy to manage, and looking at your numbers regularly so you always know where you stand. The peace of mind you'll gain is a wonderful gift to yourself and honors your hard work.

For so many of us, taking care of our business is centered around getting clients, serving clients, and doing good in the world. *Managing* our business is secondary. Perhaps you don't even think of yourself as a businesswoman. Maybe the word "business" brings up images of men in suits and sterile, white offices – places you do *not* want to spend your time. I totally get wanting to shy away from that vision of your work. Having spent years there, I can tell you it's not my vision for my business, either. You should definitely build your business in ways that brings you joy. You want to get up excited to dive into it in the morning, and feel content from having done a good day's work when you go to sleep. The beauty of being your own boss – whether you're a coach, a creative professional, a marketing whiz, or a crack virtual assistant – is that you get to choose how things are done and where you go with your business. This is a wonderful, exciting process, and I hope it's one you enjoy.

If you're here reading this book, however, I'm guessing that managing your finances is an area that's not quite as fun and enjoyable for you. You know you need to be doing something about your money, but you don't know where to start or how to feel confident with your current financial systems. Taking care of your books is usually pretty far down on the list of "tasks I love to do in my business." I mean, if we're calling it a "task," that tells us right off the bat how we feel about it, right? Like I have my laundry phobia, you may have similar feelings about managing your business finances. You may not even know exactly why you feel the way you do. You just know you've mentally got a big, red X in front of the word "accounting." Maybe you'd rather spend your efforts more on making money than managing it, and bookkeeping seems like a poor use of your time.

Whatever your reason for considering managing your books a task, understanding *what* to do and *when* to do it can alleviate a lot of the anxiety that comes from having a murky relationship with your finances. Even if you're not particularly interested in counting every penny or understanding the ins and outs of investment strategies, when your books are clean and you know your numbers, you can step into the role of a true business owner —someone who's comfortable taking a hard look at all aspects of her business, because she's committed to being exceptional in all areas (even the ones she'd rather not have to mess around with). Believe it or not, that "clean laundry" feeling is even better when it's your finances we're talking about, and I want you to have it.

Whether you like to think of yourself as an entrepreneur or not, if you "sell your brain" for a living and people pay you for your time and energy, then you're in business. That means you need to somehow manage your finances. As you read through the following chapters, try to envision your finances as a neatly folded stack of clean sheets. That tidy basket of goodness can give you the confidence you need to make smart, educated decisions about your business.

We're going to look at how to get paid for your work, how to put your cash to best use and manage your expenses, and how to build a budget and take control of your financial future – instead of letting it control you through worry, stress, and fear. Finding your own financial *Zen* starts right now.

While you're learning ways to handle your money strategically, keep the end game in mind. The process of money management may seem less-than-stellar at times, but as you gain know-how and proper tools you can pen a new narrative that's right for you. You can take a new look at the story you've been telling yourself about dealing with money being "hard," or "boring," or not for you, turn it toward the positive and free yourself to become the "real" businesswoman you're meant to be: successful, confident, and clear about your path.

Like putting on your favorite pair of pants, fresh out of the dryer, managing your finances can make you feel clean and ready. It's totally worth having to do a load of laundry to get there.

Chapter 1

The Money Mind Trip

"One's philosophy is best not expressed in words. It is expressed in the choices one makes... and the choices are ultimately our responsibility."

–Eleanor Roosevelt

f you've picked up this book, it's because you want to learn how to manage your business's finances in a way that's right for you and how to use your accounting to help you grow. The growth you want may be in revenue, profit, or simply as a human being through education. These are all superb reasons. And we'll dig into the details soon, I promise. But first I want to talk a little bit about fear. Specifically, the financial night sweats.

It took me a long time to own up to my own money discomforts and take responsibility for them. In terms of finances, I had a lot of baggage and I didn't realize it was weighing me down until I started to truly understand how money works, both in my personal life and in business. I wound up walking my personal and business financial paths in tandem, although for many people one comes before the other (or *because* of the other). But before I really started down that path, whenever I thought about money, I felt a mix of trepidation and hope. I longed for financial stability, and, if I'm honest, wealth, but I was fearful because I didn't really understand how to go from living from paycheck to paycheck to truly feeling an abundance of money. I was constantly feeling like the bottom was going to drop out and I'd be right back in the hungry days.

Tony Robbins wrote: "Shame. Fear. Guilt. Power…. These are just a few of the common emotions we associate with money. We have trained our brains to react to financial circumstances with those emotions. We make these choices unconsciously, and therefore we often select emotions that do not serve us in a productive way." When we see our choices clearly, we can change our reactions and unconscious thoughts about money. We're emotional beings and it's impossible to make significant changes in our habits without first addressing our feelings.

Do you want to learn how to better manage your business's finances? Spectacular! This is one of my favorite subjects (and hopefully it'll be one of yours soon, too). To get there, we need to flush out some personal and emotional realities. So, let's start by talking a little bit about how you perceive money.

Fear of Failure

Here's the truth of the matter. For me, and for many women I talk to, there is a fear of failure at the heart of financial discomfort. What happens if you really dig down deep and learn the ins and outs of money management, *and you still fail?* It can feel safer never to dig into your finances at all. I mean, if you're basically doing alright without really knowing what you're doing, why rock the boat? It can be terribly difficult to be honest enough with yourself to recognize what's truly driving your financial choices.

The good news is that you've already taken the first step toward clarity. You've chosen to learn more about your business and how money works. You're interested in finding out ways to make your financial life easier and ensure success in your ventures. Even better? You have me in your corner as your financial guide. It's difficult to make major life shifts without help, and facing your financial fears is no exception. I love helping people start swinging at those money monsters in their closets and ultimately defeating them. My experiences with happy, confident clients has also proven that acquiring knowledge and using information to springboard your financial journey works. It's a smart approach and you're on the right track.

Now, what if you're not really feeling like fear is part of your financial journey? Do you just want to learn best practices and know exactly what to do and when? Many readers may be in this position, as well. If you're thinking that emotional reflection doesn't have a place in a financial training book, I ask you to read the rest of this chapter with an open mind. Do the exercises and see what comes up. You may be surprised with what you learn.

A Story of Transformation

When Barb first came to me, financial fear and discomfort were driving everything about her life. She had left a decent job in the medical industry to start a business as a wellness coach. Barb absolutely loves her work and brings an incredible, positive energy to everything she does. But she didn't have good money habits. She admitted to compromising her financial integrity for the sake of her business and was desperate for things to start moving so she could work her way out of the hole she'd fallen into.

Now, Barb will be the first person to take responsibility for what happened in her financial life. She is very aware that she may have made some decisions that weren't the best for her bank account, but she felt they were 100% necessary for her growth as a coach and entrepreneur. She didn't realize it, but she had been doing a spiritual cost-benefit analysis every time she signed up for a new program or undercharged a client. In our first conversation, she told me, "Liz, I have no idea what I'm doing. This is just happening." Of course, Barb was making money decisions all along, they just weren't completely aligned with the smart business woman she wanted to be.

Knowledge became the cornerstone of our work together and in the beginning much of it revolved around her emotional relationship with money. As a young woman without many resources, Barb had managed against all odds to build a good life for herself. She's the kind of person who will always land on her feet and isn't afraid to jump at new opportunities. But she admits she is at a loss when it comes to good money management. Her experience told her she could be successful, but she felt deep insecurity about how she handled her finances.

Barb is a huge reader and when we started working together, she told me she had *Personal Finance for Dummies* sitting, unopened, on her bedside table. She knew she needed to deal with her money situation and, in buying the book, was admitting she wanted to learn. But she wasn't quite ready to get started. Her fear was still holding her back.

Let's be honest. Facing ourselves in the mirror, with our personal truths staring us down, is difficult. It's exceptionally hard work. Barb was courageous enough to admit that to herself and to "go all in" with me to learn how to manage her money better. In the process, she let go of her financial self-doubt and decades of misconceptions. She now feels she's the smart, financially savvy entrepreneur she envisioned herself being. Barb saw a gap in her knowledge and found a way to bridge it so she could truly take her finances – personal and business – to the next level.

Today, I'm happy to say Barb is thriving as a business woman and feels an amazing sense of accomplishment from doing the work she needed to do to move into a positive financial mindset. You can, too.

Fear Comes in All Shapes and Sizes

There are many ways that financial fear shows up for new (and not-so-new) business owners. It can be blatant or stealthy, but it's always there. In one way or another, fear is at work as you build your business. Sometimes, fear remains long after you've established yourself as a successful business owner.

One story I like to tell is about my friend Rachael. She's a psychologist who's had a successful practice in my town for over 15 years. She works the schedule that she wants, making time for her young family and for activities she enjoys. In many ways, she's "made it" as an entrepreneur. She has an office manager who handles all the paperwork and she makes enough to take home a regular, healthy paycheck.

I asked Rachael once about her business finances. Were they strong? Did she feel good about her numbers? Did she have plans for growth? Her answer took me aback. "Liz," she said, "I just don't want to know." She legitimately couldn't face her bookkeeping and had zero desire to understand how her business finances worked. I was floored, but I didn't say anything. Despite being a business owner for nearly two decades, Rachael isn't ready to face her financial fears. Some people embrace the challenge and want to take their businesses to the next level; some people don't. It doesn't mean you can't build a profitable business, but it's hard to grow and truly meet your wildest dreams without knowing – and nurturing – your numbers. If you're here, you're taking the steps you need to understand how money works and how you can use that knowledge to grow your business.

There may also be times when you're doing the right things to deal with your fear and you still have tough experiences. The very first client I signed as a brand-new contact came to me because she was trying to face her financial discomforts. Tavia had just started her spiritual coaching business nine months earlier and had some questions about her business. She'd had a good working relationship with an accountant in the past for her personal finances, but that woman retired, so she was looking for someone to help her navigate her new business.

Tavia went to a local accountant to get some help, thinking that a licensed professional could point her in the right direction and answer her questions about how to set up her books so she knew where she stood financially. She gave this man the perfect opportunity to become a long-term client. She was facing her financial fears and trusting him to take care of her. He failed monumentally. This accountant talked down to her, using language full of acronyms and making her feel stupid. (Those are her words, not mine.) Needless to say, she didn't feel better about her business after that meeting. And she had to pay $150 for the 30-minute privilege!

Experiences like this often lead us to decide that business finance is over our heads, complicated and confusing. Not meant for mere mortals. Nothing is further from the truth! Luckily, Tavia knew she was smart enough to figure her finances out and didn't give up. Eventually, we connected and now she feels great about her business. She knows how to make smart financial decisions, and is confident in her abilities as an entrepreneur. Asking for help – from the right person – and being open to learning guided her there.

Here's what stories like Tavia's tell us: When we hide from our finances and allow fear of the unknown to drive our money narrative, we feel overwhelmed, lost, and out of sync. When we learn how money works and apply those principles to our own life, we can open doors (internal and external) that we didn't know existed. You truly can move *from zero to Zen* with relatively little effort. It doesn't have to be hard, and everyone I've ever met is capable of doing it. Which means you are, too.

I also know that identifying your stress, worry or fear and facing it straight on is a fantastic way to release that financial tension and move to the next level. So let's talk a little more about the entrepreneurial transition and how it relates to fear.

Earner to Non-Earner to Owner/Earner

The transition from employee to entrepreneur looks different for everyone, but there are three primary stages we all go through. If you ask your friends or connections who have successfully started their own businesses, I'd bet they'll agree with me. Get them talking about their experiences; you'll find yourself in the middle of a lively conversation.

The Earner

When you work for someone else as an employee, you are an Earner. For most small business owners, the process starts here. You have a decent enough job, you've developed a level of expertise in your work, and you bring home a regular paycheck that you can count on to support yourself financially. It might not be as big as you'd like, but you can make do.

Or maybe you have no money worries, but the work doesn't excite you. You're in a space where you're not exactly happy but not exactly ready to make a leap to something new, either. You've successfully established yourself as a high-level Earner.

In the Earner stage, money is dealt with on a personal level. You might be living paycheck to paycheck or you may have a great retirement plan already in place. Either way, your financial focus is probably on what you bring home and how you spend it. Most people live in this place their entire working lives. And don't get me wrong, it can be a great place to be. But if you're reading this book now, it's because you've moved past the Earner stage into what I like to call the Entrepreneur's Adventure.

The Non-Earner

When you make the leap to starting your own business, you're taking on a lot of new things. And if you're like most people, you have high ideals and goals about what your business will bring you, including a lot of money. When you start your business, it can be very exciting and the opportunities seem endless. It's a fun time. If you're at the beginning of your Entrepreneur's Adventure, take a minute to sit back and enjoy the energy you're creating. You've gone out on a limb and you're on an adrenaline rush of "new."

There are lots of great things about this phase, but there are some negatives we should discuss too, so you're not blindsided when the bottom drops out. It happens for everyone. At some point in your new business, as you transition away from being an Earner, you'll earn less than you once did. Again, everyone will come to this in a different way. Perhaps you start your business on the side and build it up until you can quit your 9-5 job. Or maybe you don't have a choice and you *need* to make this new venture work... like, yesterday. Whatever your situation (past or present), there's a point where you will have some level of financial worry surrounding your business. You've taken on a huge commitment by starting a business and there will be at least one situation – more likely many – when you're not sure where the next client is coming from or how you're going to pay for that new training you *really* want to take so you can grow your business.

Starting your company, working hard to generate leads and get money coming in is your #1 priority in the Non-Earner stage. For most of us, this phase means that we're spending more than we're bringing in and that can be a very scary space.

When I was in the Non-Earner stage, I was regularly having nightmares about not being good enough, in one way or another. I would wake up frantically trying to remember where I'd left my keys so I could get on the road to bring my homework to my teacher, but I'd keep getting interrupted by random people showing up at my house... and on and on. It took a while for me to realize that these stress dreams were really all money-driven. In my waking life, I was pushing so hard to start generating income that it was bleeding into my dream world.

Being a Non-Earner after having been a successful Earner (sometimes for decades) can be terrifying. You start to question everything. Can you really do this? What if the business fails? Will people want to work with you? How will you support yourself between now and when you've achieved success?

In this morass of self-doubt, it can be easy to slip into a frenetic mode where you're shooting at multiple moving targets. You may find yourself buying into every new process or product out there in an effort to alleviate the discomfort. You may be thinking, "If I could find someone to tell me what to do, or buy the right system, this would all be easy and work out."

Unfortunately, even if you could find that magic person or miracle product, it wouldn't necessarily release these feelings of fear and doubt. Until you face your financial roadblocks – the things that trigger you when you're at your lowest – it's hard to successfully move through the Non-Earner phase. Even when your business is making money, you may feel it's never enough because you haven't processed what money means to you.

The goal for everyone in the Non-Earner phase is to get out of it as quickly as possible. We all hope for exceptional growth in short order so we can leave this uncomfortable space and move into a more successful one. One where money is coming in and we're able to pay ourselves *and* have a viable business. But keep in mind, that discomfort has a place: It alerts you to change. You can take that uncertainty and learn from it, even as you're working hard to get past it.

I only occasionally start working with clients in the Non-Earner stage, primarily because it's hard to wrap your mind around hiring someone to help you with your money when you're not making any money. And to be honest, it's not always the most effective time to do this work. Don't get me wrong, if you're in this phase and doing everything you can to move out of it, and want to level up your financial know-how at the same time, I say "Let's do it." It's never too early to start learning about how money can work for you. Just don't beat yourself up if you didn't focus on this part of your business right out of the gate. Everyone comes to this work in different ways, and it's important to focus on your finances at a time that's right for you, when you can get the most out of it.

The Owner/Earner

If you've already transitioned to this final phase, that means you're making money. Woohoo! It's exhilarating to bring revenue into your business and take care of your commitments – including your commitment to yourself. In this stage, you're paying your bills and putting money into your own pocket. You've made it through the hardest part of the Entrepreneur's Adventure. When you get here, take a moment to celebrate. You've achieved what many people dream of and never find: Being in charge of your own destiny and having the skills to make your life exactly what you want it to be. Pretty heady stuff. Enjoy it!

Just the other day, I reminded a client to stop and smell her financial roses. She was anticipating seeing $30,000 hit her account, the payment being the culmination of many months of work with a national organization (and the equivalent of her entire profit from the previous year). Sam is just ramping up into the Owner/Earner phase and, like many of us, was quick to dismiss this major accomplishment. In her mind, she'd already moved on to booking the next client and paying attention to her new horizon. I asked her to just sit with her win for a second. I asked her how she was going to celebrate, suggesting she do something fun for herself. At first she wasn't sure, but, as we talked more, Sam's face relaxed into a smile and she let herself take a moment to *feel* the beauty of reaching the top of this particular mountain.

If you're like most people, the full transition to thinking of yourself as an owner likely takes some time. If your work history was primarily as an employee (even if you rose through the ranks to management), it can be hard to be ultimately responsible for an entire business. Being an Owner/Earner, especially if you're a one-woman show, means that you are now the "buck stops here" lady. All your success and all your failure rides on your shoulders. That responsibility can be a lot to carry and sometimes it can be downright overwhelming. It can distract you from stopping to celebrate your successes.

As you begin to truly embrace the ownership concept, fear and discomfort may continue to crop up. You want to grow but it will involve taking on debt. Uncomfortable. You hire staff and now are responsible for their livelihoods as well as your own. Uncomfortable. There are lots of areas that may trigger your financial fears, even when your business is running strong and money is pouring in. But if you have the motivation to have made it this far, you definitely can learn how to take these new hurdles in stride, even with delight.

The Truth About Money

While we all bring our personal financial baggage to our businesses, here's the reality about money: It's just a tool. There is no bad or good about it. It simply is. Somewhere along the way we learn to place value judgments on it. "I hate money," someone may say, but they may feel that way because they believe they don't have enough of it or they simply don't understand how it works.

On the other hand, if you're thinking that money is going to solve all your problems, it's time to take a step back and look at where that particular belief comes from. Because chances are good that when you reach the next financial plateau with your business, your problems are still going to be there waiting for you. So, money isn't all good, either. The trick is learning to separate your emotional beliefs about money from the reality that money is a tool you can use to achieve your goals. You only need to learn how to use it.

Achieving Financial Clarity

I have a client, Nancy, who realized well before we started working together that she had quite a lot of financial fear and negative emotions surrounding money. Through her own personal work, she started checking in with herself at the end of the day. She asks herself, "What good thing has money brought me today?" This one simple question helps her identify the positive as well as the negative beliefs about money in her life. It's made it much easier to manage her thoughts in a way that fits with her mental road map. It works for her business mindset as well as in her personal life. She's just on the brink of transitioning to the Owner/Earner phase, and this exercise helps her acknowledge her fears and redirect her negative thoughts by focusing on the benefits of money more than the lack of it. I encourage you to try it for yourself; it's a powerful tool.

There's another exercise I do with all my financial training clients that helps us start the conversation about their feelings surrounding money. It's often eye-opening as they begin to recognize their money patterns and start looking at them in a new way. I ask them to spend a week paying attention to money as they go about their normal routines, to get a sense of how it flows in their business. It's important to do this without judgment or expectations. Simply pay attention to the movement for a few days. No guilt and no change in habits.

Money is an integral part of your life and this exercise helps you become aware of it on a conscious level. There is no good or bad; it just "is." Most clients think this is an interesting process and some find it difficult to stick with. When that's the case, there are usually some significant mental blocks to work through. Ultimately, observing the movement of their money really helps our discussions about money management take off.

REFLECTION QUESTIONS

1. How is money flowing in and how does it feel?
2. How do you decide to spend it? Is there a process you go through?
3. What are you feeling as you watch money move through your life?

EXERCISE
Financial Clarity

The next step I like to take with my clients is to start identifying how they might want to change their financial narrative. They identify three ways they want to stop thinking or feeling about money – for themselves, in their relationships, and in their business – and what they want to replace them with. For example, they may say, "I don't want to worry about my retirement anymore," and instead they make a commitment to funding their Roth IRA to the maximum this year. They identify why the new attitude is important ("I want to feel good about my future") and when they plan to accomplish the goal ("by October of this year").

Do this for yourself: Come up with three new clarity goals for each of the three categories – personal, relationship, and business. Write them down or put them in a spreadsheet to track it. You'll be surprised how much easier it'll be to focus on your finances, when you've redirected the conversation from the negative to the positive. It helps you establish your *why* for this financial work, which can make it all the more satisfying.

I recommend you do this exercise starting today. You can keep reading forward, but you'll build a more solid financial foundation for yourself if you go create your clarity goals before you dive into the bookkeeping details we'll discuss later.

The Take-Away

You know that saying "Money is power?" Many of us shy away from thinking of ourselves as powerful; it makes us very uncomfortable. We don't want to be seen as too aggressive, money-hungry, or demanding. Often, we simply don't want to be *seen* at all, at least in the realm of finance. We shy away from it, hide from our numbers, and are fearful we'll get it wrong. There's another saying I'm sure you know: "Knowledge is power." And that's what can truly set you free. Learning can allow you to recraft your relationship with money – and with power – into something supportive, positive, and liberating.

I'll bring up this theme of "information will set you free" throughout the book. Recognizing your financial roadblocks and addressing any emotional discomfort you have around money is an important first step in learning to manage your finances. This may sound very "woo woo" for a financial how-to book, but it's true. Spend some time paying attention to how you perceive money, in your personal life as well as in your business. When you can take the emotional response out of your financial decisions, you're empowered to make smart decisions for your business: Decisions based on solid data and sound reasoning. This is the arena we'll spend the most of the rest of our time in, in small, manageable bites. Little pieces of information that will ultimately set you free.

Now, let's get you learning how to take better care of your finances.

Chapter 2

My Own Less-Than-Shiny Yellow Brick Road

"To fulfill a dream, to be allowed to sweat over lonely labor, to be given a chance to create, is the meat and potatoes of life. The money is the gravy."

– Bette Davis

I came to my financial understanding late in the game. I was in my 30s before I began to feel comfortable with how money works. Considering I had been successfully supporting myself for a decade at that point, it feels a little shameful to admit. And the funny thing was that I had no idea.

I had no idea how much I was missing and how much better I could manage my finances. I thought, like many people do, that I was doing everything right and it turned out I only had the smallest tip-of-the-iceberg understanding of how money really worked. There was a whole world out there waiting to be explored. A world that would teach me lessons that made my life easier and gave me more confidence in myself. But I didn't know that yet.

We Don't Talk About Money

Many of us were raised with the unspoken rule that money isn't discussed at the dinner table. Or maybe at all. I don't remember talking about money, but I do remember us feeling stressed about it.

Both of my parents are medical professionals. They're smart people. Educated people. People who taught me how to be of service in the world and how to love learning in any form. They showed me that it's not about the paycheck, it's about the work itself.

They also taught me very little about managing my money, making strategic career decisions, or how to navigate adulthood in a financially savvy way. Even though my dad is an entrepreneurial doctor, with several business ventures still in operation today, I certainly never learned how business finance worked when I was growing up.

My parents come from a generation that did better than the one before, which had done better than the one before that, and I'm not sure it occurred to them that my siblings and I might not effortlessly do the same. I also think they fell under that seductive, false spell that leads us, as parents, to believe that everything in our own head must automatically have transferred to our children's brains upon conception. Sadly, it's not true for my kids and it wasn't the case for me. I didn't learn the bare bones of balancing a checkbook until a class in high school. I had a vague idea that racking up debt was bad, but I really didn't know how to manage a credit card.

So, while my parents were each successful in their own way, I came into adulthood with a poor understanding of how to make money and how to manage it well. I certainly had no thought that I would one day need to understand financial management for my own business.

College Tanked My Credit

Okay, I have this story that I love and hate to tell. It's the story of how I totally screwed up my credit in college. I'm not even sure my parents know this happened, I was so embarrassed about the whole situation. It's not actually my college's fault, of course, it was all me being young and ill-informed about money.

Like many 18-year-olds, my first experience with credit cards came in the first week of freshman year. There was a table manned with two ladies from Citi Card in our student center and they were giving out free water bottles if you signed up for a credit card. It seemed like it would be handy to have a credit card as an "adult" in college, so a few minutes of my time and a signature later, I was the proud owner of a brand new $1,000 credit limit and a nifty blue jug.

I had no idea what I was doing. This isn't one of those stories of complete and total financial despair brought on by random, reckless spending. I used it for books and to float until the next check came through from my student work-study contract. That part never got terribly out of hand. However, at the time I didn't truly understand the impact of only paying the minimum due, and that card was riding close to maxed out for a good chunk of my college years.

The second piece of my bad credit puzzle came in the form of bounced checks. I was in the common habit of living paycheck-to-paycheck like most students, but I obviously missed the elective on financial timing. I continually expected the money I deposited to be immediately available in my account. In those days, banks didn't give you a $100 buffer of "good faith" money upon deposit like they do today.

You'd think I would have learned the first time and moved on with a better outlook. Nope... I was living hand-to-mouth enough that it kept happening. I just figured it was my fault and I was paying the price with the fees I was incurring. I was in a habit that I couldn't seem to break, but I figured it would all come out in the wash eventually.

And it did... timing and poor choices caught up with me when, just before graduation, my bank sent me a letter saying they were closing my account due to too many overdrafts. I was stunned. Let me tell you, having a financial institution tell you to take a hike is an emotional slap in the face. I wanted to curl up in a ball and cry and pretend it never happened, because really, what kind of person screws up something so simple?

These days, I know that this kind of thing happens a lot, and it doesn't mean the people it happens to are inherently bad or unworthy. At the time, though, losing my account felt like big-time failure. But, I was going to close that account soon anyway, so I would just start over when I moved a few weeks later.

Only one hiccup in that brilliant plan. It turns out when you have an account closed by a bank due to poor money choices, other banks aren't lining up to give you a second chance. I was told by a nice lady at Wells Fargo that it would be seven years before this bad credit was removed from my record, but if I didn't incur additional black marks to my name, in three years they might be able to let me open a new checking account. With the proper record of steady income and payment of bills, and severe restrictions, of course. I think I may have made it to my car before the tears started.

I was reluctant to tell anyone about it. I couldn't bring myself to ask my parents for help. Luckily, I did confide in a friend and she offered to be my bank. She actually served as my own personal bank – free of charge – for the 36 months it took me to convince Wells Fargo I was worth their gamble as a customer. I would sign over my paychecks to her and once a month we would sit down and she would write checks out for my utility bill, my rent, and my credit card. She was, and is, a saint. I hope everyone reading this book has someone like her in your life.

This story has a happy ending, thankfully. Eventually, I was able to open an account and begin establishing good credit. By my mid-20s, I was back to handling my finances without needing a middle man. I still didn't know much, and often still spent more than I was making, but I figured it would all work out in the end… and it eventually did. I tell you this story because it's important that you know that I've been there. We all have varying degrees of financial discomfort in our past (or present) and wherever you are on your financial journey, know that I've been somewhere similar, too.

Fast Forward to My Frugal Husband

In 2004, when I met the man who would become my husband, I was making $50,000 a year plus room and board. (There are benefits to working with your parents when you haven't lived nearby for a very long time and they want you to come home from Prague.) I enjoyed this cushy position for about 18 months before I met my husband.

And, somehow, I still had $9,000 in credit card debt, plus student loans to pay off, plus I bought a new car on loan. Hello? You'd think I would have learned something along the way. But no, I liked nice things and I wanted what I wanted *now*. A very Id-oriented, childlike approach to money, but, as I said, I really didn't know any better.

My husband, on the other hand, is about as long-term a thinker as you can find. Plus, he's amazingly frugal. Even his own parents make fun of how tight-fisted he is. Having lived with him for over a decade, I can tell you he does not like waste. And spending money on something you don't need is pretty high on the no-no list.

As you might imagine, we struggled the first few years of our lives together to reconcile my spendthrift ways and his ultra-conservative approach to money. I like to think we've both learned something over the years and have come to a good, balanced place. We probably each think we've shifted more than the other, but I will say that he has gifted me with the desire for good money management and with finding joy in saving. He's the reason I now love to talk about finances and how to make money work for you.

I Grabbed an Opportunity

Living with my husband, personal finances finally started to make sense and I was well on my way to being in great shape paying down debt. I was beginning to understand where I was comfortable living in terms of money. Even though I was responsible for the day-to-day bookkeeping of the family business, however, I still had very little understanding of how a business runs best. Then, in early 2006, I made a job change and was lucky enough to get hired at a local engineering firm. That's when my business financial understanding really took off.

I left the title Director of Operations to become Administrative Assistant at this new job. By the time I left the company, I was Business Manager, Vice President of Finance, Corporate Secretary, and Partner. As I moved through those roles, I learned a great deal about running a professional services firm, how money can work for and against you, and ways to maximize your finances to grow a business.

How I Learned the Nitty-Gritty of "Selling Your Brain"

I worked exceptionally hard for several years, moving up in the firm and enrolling in an MBA program. At the same time, I was invited to buy into the business and participated in a successful ownership transition. Becoming a partner and taking over as business manager for a multi-million-dollar firm is a great trial-by-fire way to learn how to manage business finances.

It turns out that coaching, consulting, and professional service businesses – people who "sell their brains" for a living – are different from other kinds of businesses. There's no inventory. There's an office and there are vendors, and much of the accounting is the same, but certain parts of the bookkeeping are treated differently. I learned all the ins and outs of this type of financial system in my decade with the firm. I was given wonderful learning opportunities and the responsibility for being the go-to person for staff, vendors, and clients. I was a problem solver and I loved it. I had never pictured myself as a business manager, much less a business owner, but it fit me well and I was excited about my future with the company.

Life Took a Turn

Want to know what happens when you get married, start a new career, have two kids 19 months apart, buy into and successfully transition ownership of a business, and get your MBA all within 6 years? You get sick. Like, really sick.

At least that's what happened for me. It turns out I spent a long time running on an adrenaline high as I was learning all this new stuff and doing all these things that I thought I was "supposed" to be doing. Like many women out there, I was great at presenting a certain face to the world, and I wasn't even really aware of 1) what I truly wanted and 2) that I was wrecking my health to maintain that façade. I looked great on the surface but I tanked my system in the process.

Enter the "mystery illness." In October 2012, I came down with what felt like a bacterial infection. You know that feeling like you've been run over by a bus and thrown into a brick wall at the same time? Antibiotics didn't help and, when things didn't resolve, I saw specialists and had more tests, including a spinal tap and two MRIs. Everything came back normal. They couldn't figure out what was wrong with me. I worked as much as I was able, sometimes only an hour or two a day, feeling a little better but not truly well. Eventually, I was given a "good luck with the rest of your life, sorry we couldn't help you" by the medical establishment and left to my own devices.

Being the data junkies that we are, my husband and I both spent hours looking for answers on the internet. I read dozens of books, searching for a name for my fatigue, aches, and general malaise. In the meantime, I was fighting to "get back to normal" so I could reclaim my place at the table in my firm and work full time again. I was so driven I even managed to finish my last MBA class in the first few months of being ill. I was determined to complete it and thought if I could just get that part done, life would get easier. In the back of my mind, as we were spending more and more money on health-related costs not covered by insurance, a major financial fear was growing. How was I going to support my family with this illness... whatever it was?

A Seed Is Planted

A few years later, still struggling with my health and striving to do my best at work, I jumped at the chance to attend a business development conference for A/E (Architecture/ Engineering) managers in Chicago. I really love conferences, even though air travel and long days often set me back health-wise. But the trade-offs seemed worth the dive in energy that I knew would come after I got home. Bonus? I could take an extra day and visit with my best friends from college, who just happen to live in Chi-town.

While with those friends, my first thoughts about what is now my business came bubbling up. One of my friends had recently opened his private practice as a psychiatrist and, because he's a big-picture thinker, his wife had taken up the bookkeeping reins. And they found themselves learning business finances the hard way – by trial and error.

They were about 18 months into the new practice, and they had just come to terms with how taxes worked. They felt there was all this information they *should* know but didn't. She worked on the bookkeeping daily, but there were areas that could use some fine tuning, like how to deal with patients who weren't paying on time.

Somehow, we ended up talking about the practice and I gave them a few tips based on my experience. It was at that point when the wife turned to me and asked, "Do you want to do this instead of me?" That's when I realized 1) I could help my friends out, who had often helped me in the past, and 2) if they were having these problems, perhaps other people were struggling with finances as well. Something to ponder.

I hadn't really been looking for an exit strategy from my career. Remember, this was the job I was going to retire from, the one I'd put my blood, sweat, and tears into. But as I continued to deal with my "mystery illness" it was getting harder to maintain my energy. My partners were extremely flexible, given the circumstances, allowing me to work as best I could and often from home, but I was feeling more and more isolated. At the time of my Chicago visit, I didn't know anything except I wasn't happy. Something had to change, but I wasn't quite ready to face that reality yet.

Life Got Uncomfortable and I Got Serious

Within a couple of months, I'd started working with a new practitioner who recommended another battery of tests that included the gold standard for Lyme testing. I'd tested negative three or four times already, but I took on the $500 expense and sent blood to a lab in California where, lo and behold, it turned out that *Borrelia Burgdoferi* – the bacteria that causes Lyme Disease – was floating around in my system.

It was a shocking revelation. I now had a real diagnosis and I wanted to figure out how to deal with it *fast*. Lyme is a tricky disease and, if not treated immediately, it's complicated to manage. I was almost four years into the illness, so I took a month off to rest and attempt to figure out what life might look like going forward. It clearly would be quite a while before I could get back to a 40-hour work week and I was aware that my partners' patience was wearing thin. I lay in bed and started ticking through ways I might be able to earn money from home, if it came to that. I wondered if my friends in Chicago might actually hire me to help them out with their books. I knew a few people with companies that might need some financial management support. Perhaps I could cobble together something based on that?

So instead of resting during that month, I built a business. I chose the name Statera Business Solutions because *statera* in Latin means balance, value, and scales. My vision was to help small business owners take care of their books and find balance in their work, without stress or strain.

It was the best thing I ever did. At the time, I had no idea how exciting it would be to work directly with clients. My previous roles had been supportive and I didn't contact clients much, except to badger people for money or negotiate a contract. The idea of building something new was energizing, so even though I was struggling to get better and I was tiring myself out, I felt more satisfied than I had in a long time. I also didn't know that moving on professionally would be a major part of my recovery.

In a certain sense, I had to go through a major illness to realize my true potential. Since the day I started focusing on getting better and on building my business, I've never looked back. As my health returned, my vision became more specific and now I help coaches and creative professionals master their finances so they can grow an amazing business with confidence. My clients are superb at what they do but feel overwhelmed with the financial management they (begrudgingly) admit is essential for a successful business. They can focus on doing what they love with peace of mind when their finances are in order.

As part of my work, I spend time training my clients on platforms and programs that streamline their financial activities. We also talk a lot about best management practices and big picture strategy, so they can begin to understand how daily accounting relates to business growth. I like to think of myself as a financial guide, supporting and encouraging entrepreneurs to dive into their money management and demystifying the financial process through education and support.

The Take-Away

The lessons in this book are part of the training I do with my clients. Becoming familiar with the financial concepts discussed in the following pages has helped them gain confidence as entrepreneurs and take their businesses to a new level. I want to bring the same level of understanding and excitement about running a business to as many people as possible. I want to help you understand the impacts of your financial decisions, so you can make smart choices for your business. As a solopreneur or small business owner, your business and personal life tends to be intertwined, which means you're making smart choices for your life, too.

Now, let's get you started down *your* yellow brick road!

Chapter 3

The Journey from Zero to Zen

"Money speaks sense in a language all nations understand."
– Aphra Behn

O h dear, it's that time. The pile of laundry is building up and it's time to talk about how we're going to get you feeling great about your finances. You might be a little nervous. Don't worry, we'll take it slow. Like anything worthwhile, financial understanding is a process and we'll build up to it. I'm guessing that a lot of what we'll cover you're already doing, even doing much of it well. You'll be able to take the lessons and systems we'll discuss and tweak your money management just a bit to kick your financial engine into high gear.

This work can make a huge difference in how you feel about your business. A client recently told me, "Thank you for being my financial life raft! You saved me from my stress and worry about all of this, and I feel so much better about my business now." If you've been nervous about taking care of your books, finding yourself ignoring your numbers, or generally feeling unsure about your finances, I want you to know those feelings don't have to last. Financial success doesn't have to be hard, and you can do this. You can feel so confident and competent about your money, you won't even recognize yourself. You can be the entrepreneur you want to be – successful in *all* aspects of your business.

Did you know that women-owned businesses are on the rise? According to the Institute of Women's Policy Research, small business ownership by women is increasing. The number of women-owned firms has grown 68 percent since 2007, compared to 47 percent for all businesses. Overall ownership by women is about 29 percent in the US, up from 26 percent in 1997. That means more and more women are jumping into entrepreneurial waters. You are part of a great and growing tribe of powerful ladies, creating strong businesses serving themselves and others. Developing a strong financial foundation is one piece of learning to swim in those waters, to take away the fear and morph those sharks into baby guppies.

Now, there's a whole language of finance that you may or may not be fluent in. You're probably familiar with a great deal of it, and are a native speaker in parts of it. You may even have your personal finances completely locked down and solid. But I'm guessing if you've picked up this book, you're not entirely comfortable with the language of business finance. We're going to define and discuss some financial terms that will be used throughout the remaining chapters, so you can start feeling more of an expert in business money management.

To get you there, we're going to start off by looking at some basic financial terms and typical financial workflows, so you can see which model you may want to use for *your* business.

Money Talk: The ABCs of Small Business Finance

We need to go through a few brief definitions to get us started, so we're all singing from the same song sheet, as my music teacher used to say. The following are important as you delve into your books:

Assets – Did you know your business has assets? I'm sure you've heard this word before and it's pretty simple to explain. Your assets are anything of value in your business. Think of the money in your checking account and the laptop you use for work. It's anything that's cash or can be turned into cash. Your assets show up on your Balance Sheet, one of two main financial reports.

Liabilities – Your liabilities include anything for which you owe money. Do you have a credit card for your business that carries a balance? Did you take a loan to start up your business (from yourself or others)? Did you buy something and you're paying over time? These amounts you owe are called liabilities and also show up on your Balance Sheet.

Equity – You may have heard this term thrown around by investment advisors and bankers. It's one of those fuzzy words that don't have a clear meaning for most of us. For our discussions, equity will be what's left over when you subtract your liabilities from your assets. The more equity in your business, the stronger your financial standing.

Revenue – Revenue (or income) means the amount of money you bring in to your business. Typically, this means the total you have billed your clients. It's good practice to review your income numbers at least monthly and again after December 31st to have a sense of how much business you're doing throughout the year. How much revenue did you have last month? The month before? Knowing these numbers can help you develop a plan for your business.

Expenses – No brainer on this one, right? Business expenses are the costs you take on to operate your company. They may include utilities, telephone, internet, subscriptions, office supplies, legal fees, and marketing costs, to name a few. Anything that you spend to keep the lights on and your business running falls into the expense category.

Financial Report – Your business's financial reports give you an overall view of the money moving in and out of your business. These reports allow you to review your financial standing and are typically used internally to make decisions for the company. Sometimes, they may be shared with potential investors, as well. There are two main types of financial reports: the Balance Sheet and the Income Statement.

Bottom Line – This term is used in many ways in our world. From a financial standpoint, your bottom line is the total amount you've earned or lost at the end of a period of time (usually monthly or annually). Sometimes it's called Net

Profit and is used to discuss whether your profit is decreasing or increasing (a "strong bottom line in the first quarter helped ABC Company's outlook").

This is just a brief primer for the financial language we'll use throughout the book. You can do a quick Google search for "financial terms" to learn more as you get more comfortable with this kind of money talk.

Accountant vs. Bookkeeper: Which Do *You* Need?

I know there's a lot of confusion out there about what an accountant does and what a bookkeeper is. The standard dictionary definition is that bookkeepers take care of daily financial record-keeping while accountants are responsible for big picture analysis of those records.

In a nutshell, bookkeepers specialize in nitty-gritty financial activities and data entry. Many small business owners don't have the need for an in-house financial person and take care of daily transactions themselves, perhaps retaining a bookkeeper for monthly reconciliations and to review the financial reports with an unbiased eye.

On the other hand, an accountant – often a Certified Public Accountant or CPA – is a licensed professional responsible for performing financial analysis, audits, and generating tax returns for individual and business clients. They don't typically provide day-to-day financial management services, but can be called on to help identify tax ramifications of capital purchases and other strategic decisions. As a business owner, it's a good idea to have a relationship with a CPA with whom you're comfortable asking questions, even if you don't engage them to do your taxes.

As with everything, there are hybrids out there too. Many experienced bookkeepers provide higher level analysis to their clients and there also are financial management consultants who bring strategic planning and financial expertise, but who don't provide day-to-day assistance. I happen to offer both day-to-day assistance as well as higher level planning and consulting, but I don't prepare taxes (I leave that part to CPAs I've developed partnerships with over the years). Some CPAs only do taxes and don't provide strategic assistance. Sorting out exactly what type of service someone provides is important so you're not hiring someone to do one thing when they really specialize in another. If someone doesn't have experience in the area you need help with, they probably can recommend someone to you.

Not sure what kind of help you need? Having a clear picture of how your business runs can help you identify which services might be of benefit. As you continue to learn more about your business finances and develop a solid money management process, you'll begin to see where you may need help and which type(s) of financial professionals may the best fit for your circumstances.

Your Prime Directive: The Financial Equation

Okay, a lot of this is going to seem obvious, but we need to go through it just to make sure we're in step here. The basic financial equation is this: *Income minus expenses equals profit.* What does this mean for you? In your personal life, it means taking the money you earn (your *income* or *revenue*) and subtracting out what you spend (your *expenses* or *costs*) will leave you with something left over (your *profit* or *net income*). Sound familiar? Most of us spend our lives attempting to increase our revenue, so we can increase our spending on things we enjoy (vacations, toys, etc.) and hope to have something left over for retirement or savings. We may not use these terms, but the process is the same for everyone.

For many business owners, the same concept filters through in how they run their company. "Let's make a bunch more money so we can upgrade our systems, hire more help, and hopefully have something left over to put into our own pockets." There's nothing wrong with this approach, assuming your business can sustain your growth and you have a solid plan for utilizing your new cash in a way that meets your overall goals. I have no problem wanting to spend money on fun trainings or finally purchasing that cool new software platform. It's your business, enjoy it! Just make sure you spend with an eye to potential ups and downs, so you're not caught short.

Managing Your Money: Basic Financial Flow

You'll find a theme running throughout this book: *consistency*. When managing your money, establishing strategies and routines that you can perform regularly is the key to relieving that "Oh my gosh, what do I do now?!" feeling. You know the one… when you're feeling like you're forgetting something or missing a test. If you hold yourself to a financial schedule, you'll find it's easier to manage that fear because you'll always know exactly where you stand in terms of money and you won't wonder if you've forgotten to do something critical. That's rule #1 as we delve into bookkeeping basics: *be consistent*.

The flow may look something like this: Contract with your client, perform the work, bill your client, get paid, rinse and repeat. Or perhaps you're paid entirely up front and never send a bill to your client. (If that's how your business runs, this is awesome, by the way.) I've listed the business flow here according to a traditional workflow, but never fear! We'll talk about variations as we go deeper. Just know that regardless of your situation, you'll need all those steps at one point or another. For now, let's talk a little bit about more about each step, since *how* you approach them can make a difference in the health of your books (and your sanity).

Contract with Client

Do you write specific contracts for each new client or funnel them through a shopping cart? Do you include a few terms and conditions in the contract or cart? Either way, when someone decides to work with you and you provide them with a fee, you're entering into a *contract* with them. This is an area that makes many new entrepreneurs jumpy. We just want to get in there and help people (darn it!) Why do we need to go through this annoying contracting phase first? Because it's critical to your financial success. We'll talk more about the importance of your contract, so simply keep in mind that the way you start your working relationship sets the tone for everything that comes later.

Perform the Work

The second step is what we usually want to dive straight into: *the work*. Many of us start a business so we can help others, in one way or another. If you're a coach, creative professional, or consultant, your main job is to teach, train, encourage, problem solve, or otherwise establish a new level of understanding for your client in your area of expertise. Doing the work feels like a piece of cake for you. Digging in and solving problems is your playground and where you're probably most comfortable.

Bill the Client

You've done the work and the client is happy. Yay, dance party time! In the traditional business environment, you would now process an invoice in your accounting system and send it to your client for payment. What does that mean? This is when you recognize the income from your work. Depending on your financial system and invoicing capabilities, this may mean emailing an invoice to your client with a link to pay via credit card embedded in the document. Maybe you take payment information over the phone before you even get started. Perhaps you even go old school and offer terms to your clients, sending an invoice in the mail and giving them a certain timeframe to pay it.

Get Paid by the Client

This is the fun part, right? Whether you get paid up front or after you're done, getting paid by your client is a superb feeling. It's the culmination of your hard work and effort, and a very real proof of your professional worth. Who doesn't like holding a pile of cash in their hands or depositing a check into the bank? From a business flow standpoint, lots of people end their financial cycle there. But understanding how to manage your revenue, knowing where to put it and how to use it, are important for your financial health. In many ways, getting paid is the end and the beginning of the financial cycle. We'll dive into this more a bit later.

Bookkeeping Basics: Follow These Steps to Success

Now that we've gone over your general business flow, let's talk about some bookkeeping basics.

There's a pattern in your finances that, when you've mastered it, will allow you to understand exactly where you stand at any point in time. Even if you're not the person who actually does the day-to-day data entry for your business, knowing *how* it should go is important. Here are the basics steps for your financial system (and don't worry, even if you do this by hand and don't have an official bookkeeping system, the concepts still apply):

Step 1: Separate your personal and business accounts. You've probably heard this before and perhaps have already taken care of it. As a business, you're responsible for maintaining accurate records of your financial activity. Having a business-only checking account and credit card (even if they're not officially "business" accounts) goes a long way toward that goal. Your grocery bill isn't mixed up with your business travel expenses and it's way easier to collect your year-end data for tax time.

Step 2: Set up your new client in your accounting system. It's a great idea to take their legal business name, address, and both phone and email addresses. I like having at least two ways to get in touch with them, in case of internet outages or ignored phone calls. Make sure you store any personal or credit card information securely.

Step 2: Invoice for your work or enter sales receipts for payments you receive. A lot of programs help make this step easy. You can also send statements or make reminder phone calls for any invoices that haven't been paid yet.

Step 3: Pay your bills on time and in full. This helps you avoid paying interest charges or late fees. If it's not always possible, don't stress! Just be aware of the costs.

Step 4: Review your numbers monthly and develop a plan to pay yourself. Knowing how much you can take out of your business is a great feeling!

Step 5: Pay your quarterly federal and state taxes. If you do this regularly, you'll be less likely to be shocked come tax time. Plus, you can avoid penalties for not making estimated payments.

Step 6: Prepare year-end tax reporting forms and file your taxes. Get help from an accountant or tax preparation specialist if you're not comfortable doing this yourself.

The important thing is to get into a habit with your finances that allows you to know exactly where you stand at any point. Not used to looking at your numbers? It's like developing any other good habit. It takes time and practice. Once you start doing it regularly, you'll feel less intimidated by the work and more in control of your business.

A Story About the Half-and-Half Company

I've got a story that may help you see the benefits of consistent, thoughtful financial management. Sally was a successful health provider who, after years of doing well in her one-woman practice, decided to buy out another one-person business to gain new clients and increase her revenue. On paper, this new addition looked like a great idea. The business had a 20-year history and good name recognition in the area. The owner was looking to retire and the price was more than reasonable. All signs appeared to point to go, so Sally took on the new business, all its clients and its current work, and was off and running.

Eighteen months later, she was closing the doors on the new venture and taking a loss. Why? Two reasons: She didn't do enough due diligence to understand that the business was being phased out by online competitors and, most importantly for our conversation, she didn't make sure she had enough resources to support the new investment. Now, she didn't have much control over the first issue, other than staying on top of local advertising and guiding existing clients through the transition in a positive way.

But the second situation was completely of her own making. Because she didn't pay much attention to her own financial management, she didn't recognize that this new business required much more oversight – to manage additional help, to get clients to pay their invoices, to take care of documentation – or that there were more vendor interactions than she was used to. The steps she needed to follow were unfamiliar and she didn't take that into account.

You'll hear me repeat this throughout the book: This isn't rocket science, but good accounting does take attention. Sally expected the money to flow easily into the new service and thought she could seamlessly entwine it with her current system, while skipping some of the critical steps. Unfortunately, the two businesses were not as alike as she had thought and Sally found herself having to support the new venture with her established business. This went on for about a year before she decided to throw in the towel and close that piece of her company. Sally took a loss and if you ask her about it, she'll tell you it was all because the market was shifting and she got the short end of the stick.

I view this with a different light. When it comes to financial management, spending time understanding how money flows in and out of your business is one major key to your success. Sally didn't truly "get" how her money worked – not in her original business or in the new venture she took on. For years she'd skated by, occasionally looking at her bank statements and giving her receipts to her accountant at the end of the year. She generated great income and so didn't often look at how much she was spending for her business. When she wanted a new laptop, she bought one. She went to as many conferences as she liked and took plenty home for her personal use.

When Sally took the same approach to the new business, it just didn't cut it. Suddenly, she had to manage an extra person, had to write off half of her invoices because she never followed up with clients for payment, and there was no room for extra spending in the budget. Hindsight is 20-20 of course, but I like to think that given the proper attention to her financial management, Sally's adventure into growth could have been successful.

The main point? Learning what needs to happen in your finances and staying on top of them can make the difference between success and failure. Your business will flourish if you make time to manage your finances.

REFLECTION QUESTIONS

1. What does my financial picture look like today?
2. What do I want it to be?
3. How will I get there?

EXERCISE
Am I Ready for Success?

Take a few minutes and think about your financial activities today. What do you do on a regular basis? What do you do every once in a while? Do you skip any of the six steps we talked about? Where do you feel most confident and where do you know you need some help? Developing goals for your financial management will help you achieve them quickly and with lasting results. Take a few minutes to consider what's been holding you up in your bookkeeping and where you're feeling confident.

The Take-Away

We've covered a lot of new language and information and you may be sweating a little, wondering just what you've gotten yourself into here. Don't worry. You've got an overview and we'll keep walking through all the pieces of your financial puzzle together. The next chapters break down the basics into easy to manage, digestible bites. If things get overwhelming, you can simply take a break or do one of the exercises for a while instead. This often happens when I take my clients through my program and you should feel free to stop and consider now and then too. Evaluating and implementing the strategies one at a time will help them make sense and become better ingrained, so your time spent here is worthwhile. Don't be afraid to take it at your own speed; I'll be here whenever you're ready to move ahead.

Chapter 4

Happy Clients Equal a Happy You

"Money can be more of a barrier between people than language or race or religion."

– Vera Caspary

D o you ever feel that if your clients are happy, you won't be? Many of us put so much into supporting our clients, we wind up feeling short-changed, tired, or taken advantage of. I want better for you. So, I have a question: When you think of your financial flow, where does it start? Many of us think it starts by doing the work. We love connecting with clients and digging into the process, but often coming to agreement over our services can cause sleepless nights and the greying of hair. We ask ourselves "Did I ask too much?" and "Did I ask too little?" and "Will they like me?" and "Did I forget anything?"

Whether we like it or not, those questions and concerns from our inner voices can influence our client relationships. This is especially true if you're not clear about how you want to work with clients, what your expectations are, and how you're going to go about turning your work into cash, so let's spend a little time getting clear on that.

It can be hard to feel completely confident 100% of the time during the process of signing someone up to work with you. I still struggle with it myself occasionally; I probably always will. Just try to remember that if you're providing a service that someone is paying you to complete, you're technically in a contractual relationship. That's probably not how you want to think about it, is it? I know it's way more fun to focus on the warm and fuzzy feelings you share with your clients. However, here's something to consider: The best way to keep them (and therefore you) happy is with a clear understanding of what you'll provide, when you'll provide it, and how they'll pay you. In official business language, this means *a clear contract and payment terms*. Having this in place can be a great way to avoid miscommunications and hard feelings.

So, let's look at ways to establish solid financial communications. It's best if the process starts with a contract that meets both your and your client's needs. It's possible you don't work with a contract yet, and that's totally okay. We'll go through it all together step by step.

I also want to talk about various ways you can get paid for your services. Whether you send invoices and offer your clients payment terms, or simply run their credit card and prep a sales receipt, these activities are part of your client communications.

They can make or break your client's trust just as easily as a misspelled email or poorly executed coaching session, so let's help you nail this part of the accounting process. Contracts and payment terms are not as hard as they may sound and you can become a financial communication rock star with a few tweaks.

Contracts 101: Getting on the Same Page

Think of this phase like the beginning of a relationship. You see your perfect client across the sea of social media noise and your eyes lock. You meet in the middle of the room and the stars align. Thank the heavens, your perfect client decides you're the cat's meow, too! You make an offer and they accept – you're golden, right? I know this is the fun part and it can be hard to think about muddying the waters with boring contractual language and unsexy terms and conditions. Here's why it's important: What happens when the honeymoon is over and you get into your first fight? A contract can help alleviate any misconceptions about the relationship and lay out exactly what you and your client will and won't do. Without a contract in place, it's too easy to undervalue the hard work you're putting in for your client. It's also easy to fall down a rabbit hole of misunderstandings about the services you provide.

Hopefully, this isn't the first time you've considered your contract, although perhaps not using that particular word. Even if it's just a verbal understanding, you probably outline how you'll do your work and what your client will get out of it. You may already have something at least a little bit formal in place that covers your interests and spells out your working relationship. Maybe it's a document you write specifically for each project or perhaps it's the terms and conditions attached to an online program purchase. Either way, the details of your agreement are like a user's manual for your work. The agreement can be an excellent educational tool, especially if you provide services that aren't entirely understood by the client. It can be hard to explain exactly what you do, but coaches and consultants of all kinds can benefit from a well-written contract. I'd like you to consider using some variation of a formal agreement when you provide services for your clients and taking some time to consider whether you want to bury it in the checkout process or make it a part of your initial client communications, so everyone is on the same page regarding your services.

The good news is that a contract doesn't have to mean pages and pages of cold, unfriendly legalese. Go ahead and search online for "coaching contract" or "consulting contract" and you'll find a bunch of examples that you could tailor to your business. We don't have time to dive fully into the wide world of contracts here, but these are the primary things I want you to think about:

- Use your contract to establish your fee. Whether lump sum or hourly, make it very clear how much your client will pay you for your services.
- Use your contract to identify your schedule. Most people don't work indefinitely, so define the length of service. You can give yourself a buffer if that's appropriate ("The work will be completed within 4 – 5 weeks," for example). If you do ongoing work, you can

identify how you and your client terminate the work if one of you decides to call it quits.

- Use your contract to specify your terms. Are you paid up front or on a monthly basis? Do you charge interest for invoices past due? Will your clients pay you in regular installments? It's good to have these details explicitly outlined in your contract.

- Get your client to sign on the dotted line. All this discussion and work to pull a contract together is no good if your client won't agree to it *in writing*. If they won't, this is a good opportunity to figure out where the disconnect is and work through it. Sometimes the client may walk away but you'll learn something valuable from the experience.

- Don't do *any* work until the contract is signed. This seems obvious, doesn't it? You'd be surprised how many women are uncomfortable pushing for a signed contract. It's too easy to think "I like this person; they're good for it." If you're a people-pleaser, make this a part of your protocol and don't apologize. If it makes asking for a signature easier, remember that your contract isn't just to protect you, it also protects your client. It identifies both parties' responsibilities and can be a great educational tool when presented properly.

Here's what I want you to keep in mind: *your work has value*. You're giving your client something worthwhile and a contract helps you establish that. It's also a good tool to help keep yourself on track. As I'm sure you've already experienced, many times a project can get out of hand. Perhaps the client changes gears or an unexpected roadblock forces you to put in additional time. Maybe the client calls you every day with a new question and you didn't plan for that. Project management 101 tells us that anytime your scope of work changes, it's time to step back and discuss the situation with your client. Will it take you longer to accomplish their goals? Perhaps it's time to ask for more money. Additional fees? They say that something becomes true when it's written down. I don't want you eating extra costs all the time and a contract can help keep things on track.

I know it can be difficult to go back and ask for more money, and managing the work in a way that keeps you financially sound is an art form, one that takes time to learn. In the beginning, we tend to cringe when we get to this point in our relationship with a client. It's uncomfortable.

In bringing this up, I simply want you to think about how you might handle such a situation and determine your general policy for when something unexpected arises. Because it will. This is where consistency, in conjunction with a sound plan, will help you take the emotional response out of the situation and help you maintain a strong financial position for the work you're doing. And if you create a plan, it's totally fine to ignore it for a particular circumstance. The cool thing is that if you have a policy in place (at least in your mind), you can decide to adjust it on the fly as an exception for that special client... and let them know you're doing them a favor by doing so.

A Tale of Two Contracts

Here's a little story for you about the value of a well-written contract. Emily is a talented interior designer. She specializes in high-end home renovations and has gotten to the point in her career where she can be selective when choosing her clients. Emily is a real go-getter and is lucky enough to *love* her job. She makes good money and her clients rarely blink at her fees. She typically has no problem explaining what she'll be doing and her clients rave about her services, so at one time she also wasn't very diligent about her contracts. Then a client created a major problem.

This beachfront renovation was a killer project and Emily really, really wanted to land it. It was a big fee and she ignored some red flags in the negotiation process. When she sent over her proposal, the client came back with a million tweaks and "what ifs." Emily told the client they could hash it all out as the work progressed. Because she really wanted to dig in and get started, she didn't bother finalizing the contract and didn't get a written approval. The project kicked off and midway through, the client decided he wanted to go in a different direction. And he wanted Emily to start all over within her original proposal.

Obviously, this was a no-win situation. Emily didn't want to work for free – she'd already been pulling long nights trying to meet the tight schedule – but she didn't want to fight with her client, either. When she tried to talk about changing the scope of her work, the client refused to discuss it. Things got messy, lawsuits were threatened, and Emily ended up walking away $25,000 in the hole on the project. She felt *lucky* because if it had gone to court, she would have ended up paying a lot more.

Compare that to Samantha, a web designer in Phoenix. She had an equally exciting opportunity, but she made a point of developing a contract that met her and her client's needs, took the time to review it so they were both on the same page, and got everything buttoned up before she started working. When the client changed the project mid-way through, Samantha stopped working and confidently presented an additional work authorization for the change in services. Because they had discussed just such a possibility during the initial contract negotiation and it was spelled out clearly in the paperwork, the client didn't blink an eye. Samantha ended up doubling her initial fees and the client couldn't be happier.

Moral of the story? Do yourself and your client a favor by having a fair and easy-to-explain contract outlining what you will and won't do, what you'll be paid, when you'll deliver, and any additional terms and conditions appropriate for you and your industry. It can feel embarrassing to ask for these things, but getting it all down on paper is an important way to protect yourself.

Wondering what happens next? Let's talk about how to turn your hard work into cash.

To Paris With Love: Sending the Bill

This part is the best! It feels amazing to complete your work and sending the bill is the culmination of doing what you love. There are multiple ways you can ask for payment for your services. Traditionally, a business will contract for services, provide the services, and then invoice for the work. In today's online environment, sometimes steps are inverted or skipped altogether. Whatever your situation, billing for your work is where the accounting process starts. So let's talk about your various options for getting paid.

Old School: Contract – Do the Work – Invoice – Get Paid

In this payment flow, the primary thing to remember is *consistency*. Sound familiar? You want to be sure that you spell out in your contract how you'll invoice your client. I recommend you send a bill monthly if you're doing on-going work or an extended project. Set up a schedule – beginning of month, end of month, mid-month – it doesn't really matter as long as you send out bills regularly. Generate your invoice which includes your company information, your client's information, and a detailed listing of what you're billing them for. That way, your message is super clear and it's harder for misunderstandings to occur.

Your accounting program should make this effortless for you. You can set a standard message that includes a request for prompt payment and a reference to your terms, as outlined in your contract. I wouldn't recommend offering more than Net 30 (they pay you within 30 days) as a coach, and would rather see you asking for Net 10, if not Due Upon Receipt. This will encourage early payments and keeps your invoice from getting lost in a pile on the desk. Ask yourself how you can use your invoicing schedule to your best advantage.

Many service providers work in this way. When you're consistent with your invoices, it can be a great way to manage your client's expectations and offer them a little leeway in payment (i.e. they don't have to pay everything up front). This is particularly useful if you offer high value services, where your client may not be able to swing 100% of your fee at once. The downside is you may end up chasing people for money. (We'll discuss this more in the next chapter.)

New School: Contract – Get Paid – Do the Work

These days, many of us come to agreement with our clients and ask for payment up front, sometimes just over the phone. You might get paid with a check, credit card, or perhaps a bank transfer (although that's not my favorite option). Maybe you offer a training program of some kind, your client signs up and pays you with a credit card, and you're off to the races. You might give them a deal if they can pay the entire fee up front, with some (smallish) increase in price to divide payment into 3 or 4 segments. Usually, they're finished paying for your services before you're finished with the work.

This is a fantastic way to do business! You get the money right away (or as soon as your credit card/merchant provider processes it) and you don't have to remember to send invoices and follow up. While it hasn't always been the norm in consulting circles, this approach to invoicing is catching on in a variety of service-based industries. And it can certainly make your life easier.

There's one potential downside to getting paid up front – just a small one, but worth mentioning: Being paid at the beginning of a contract can lead to a "feast or famine" mentality about your money and can mess with your mind a bit. When you're getting a big chunk of change right up front, two things tend to happen. First, you're getting the reward before the work, which can have a psychological impact on how you approach your job. Sometimes it becomes easy to give a half-effort because you've already got the cash in hand. Try to be aware of this as you work with your clients. It's a good idea go above and beyond for them *because* they've trusted you enough to pay you first.

The second possible pitfall is that you don't plan well for those weeks when the money *isn't* coming in. It feels great to watch your bank account jump up overnight. It feels less great to go crazy and spend it all on fun, shiny toys and forget you need to pay for your phone bill in a couple of weeks. If you're getting paid up front, make sure you have a plan for managing your cash so you don't feel the "famine" part as severely. With a little planning, you should be able to avoid it altogether.

Keep It Simple, Seriously (KISS)

We all know the KISS acronym and we know it applies to pretty much everything. Even (or especially) keeping your clients happy. When you think about writing your contracts and planning how you'll bill for your time, really and seriously, *keep it simple*. The more complicated your language and your system, the more ways you create potential problems. Sending out a contract based on a template for another type of service? Potential problem. Invoicing sporadically or many days later? Potential problem.

Your primary goal as a woman in business is to do the work you love. But behind that is the goal to support yourself, yes? Making sure your contract and invoicing plan gets you paid in an easy, speedy fashion helps a lot. And once you've developed a flow that works for you, you can put contracts and invoicing on autopilot and you'll be able to focus on things that you enjoy, knowing that your process works *for* you, not against you.

REFLECTION QUESTIONS

1. What type of contract do you use?
2. What is your invoicing style?
3. How can your financial communications keep your clients happy?

EXERCISE
Happy Clients

In this exercise, I want you to identify the type(s) of contracts and payment terms that are right for your business. Do you have contract language in place yet? If not, now's a great time to think about what will work for you and your business. That might mean an electronic contract or language you add to your online storefront. Take some time to review your current documents if you have them. Do they fully meet your business's needs? Are they written with clear language or complete legalese? If you can't understand them, chances are good your clients won't either. As you read through it, think about your goals. You want your contract to protect you, of course, but also identify the details of your services in a way that engages your client, instead of putting them off. Make sure your contract fits *you*. And get legal guidance once you've established your templates, to make sure your contracts are doing what you need. Working with an attorney is a wonderful way to understand your agreements inside and out, so you can better answer your clients' questions. Added bonus? You'll up your entrepreneurial game.

This is also a great time to map out your billing process. How often will you send invoices? Getting paid up front? How will you manage your payments and keep yourself on track? Thinking through your steps now can make the process painless and worry-free.

The Take-Away

At the end of the day, being completely clear up front will create a happy client relationship. Put yourself in your client's shoes. You know you respond better to friendly communications than to pages of fine print. Make a point of reviewing your agreement with your client as part of your on-boarding process, so there's no confusion and even less chance of them walking away because of a misunderstanding.

Having a clear invoicing strategy that you stick with consistently will enhance your business. Not only will your client know what to expect, your financial communications will show you to be the organized, successful entrepreneur you are. Your reputation as a business owner can only benefit.

If you take nothing else away from this chapter, I hope it's this: Start as you mean to go on. Being clear right from the start with yourself and your client can make for a beautiful working relationship. Having a solid contract in place along with consistent invoicing and payment procedures will alleviate any "what do I do now?" panic. We'll look at how to streamline that process even further in the next chapter. Join me whenever you're ready.

Chapter 5

Show Me the Money!

"The two most beautiful words in the English language are 'check enclosed.'"

– Dorothy Parker

If you're like me, it probably seems like getting paid should be easy. Why do we even need to talk about it, right? You've come to an agreement, done the work, and billed your client for your services. They should have no problem paying you, right? Or if you get paid up front, you'll never be asked for a refund. Oh, I wish it were that simple. Don't get me wrong, oftentimes payment *is* just like that and your hard-earned cash flows in without much oversight. If you've set up your business properly and established the right expectations with your client, at least 90% of your income should magically roll into your checking account. You probably already have a system in place, and hopefully it won't take much to tweak it so you can get the most out of it.

I know you're wondering, "What about that other 10%?" The 2016 Atradius Payment Practices Barometer reported that "around 22% (of business respondents) either lost revenues or had to pursue additional financing from banks... to get the necessary funds to pay their own creditors." That means they had a hard time getting paid and couldn't pay their bills. Not getting paid may not seem like a big deal for your small business, but it's a problem that's discussed throughout the business community. Your cash flow can get dicey if you have to chase too many people for money. The good news is that billing is also an opportunity to move the arrow toward that magic 100% easy receipt of cash.

Let's talk about ways to avoid spending your precious time getting people to pay you, because that's hands down the worst part of being a business owner. Chasing your clients down for money is the last thing you want to be doing, and the last thing I want for you! So how do you avoid this common problem? Develop a strategy, make a plan, and prepare your communications. In today's digital world, it's especially easy to get clients to pay you – and be happy to do so – with a few well-thought-out strategies put into place beforehand. This all falls under what's called *accounts receivable* in the business world, and may sound intimidating. It's just the process of turning your invoices into cash, and it's something you're already doing, which means you're totally ready to become an expert.

The first thing to consider here is your business model, as discussed in the previous chapter. Are you following a "Do the

Work – Invoice – Receive Payment" model or a "Get Paid – Do the Work" model? Depending on your business, your strategy, planning, and preparation will differ. Feel free to skip below to whichever model best fits you and your business.

Getting Paid Strategy: Do the Work – Invoice – Receive Payment

I want to spend just a little time on this traditional model. In this scenario, your strategy centers on removing obstacles around getting your clients to pay you. That includes a clean and thoughtful contract and at least a brief discussion with your client reviewing the details of your agreement, so nothing is a surprise later. It's so much easier to bring up topics like payment terms and interest charges as a *reminder* to your client if you've covered it in the beginning. When they sign on to work with you with open eyes, it's much harder to argue that they didn't realize they needed to pay you within 30 days. This is your goal in a nutshell: use your on-boarding activities to set your payment expectations.

Your plan in this model includes deciding how and when to send out Accounts Receivable correspondence. A good rule of thumb is to send a statement to your clients with the balance they owe you at the end of each month because doing it some months and not others sends an unspoken message to your clients: *she's not paying attention*. It's also a good idea to schedule a reminder to assess finance charges (if your agreement includes it) – and process any charges regularly. These actions tell your client that you're on top of things and their payment is important.

If you've been on top of your planning, there shouldn't be too many instances where you need to track down a payment. For this, you'll want to look back at your records and make a note of which invoices haven't been paid so you know who to contact and the amount that's due. I like to review the project history to remind myself of a client's individual circumstances before I start making calls.

I like to send out a statement and follow up with a phone call 5 – 7 days later. Why not email? It's too easy to ignore. Find out if they received the statement, after first asking how they're doing and possibly making some small talk. If it's a larger organization, you may be talking to someone who fields angry collections call all day and they're usually surprised when you take an interest in them. If it's your actual client, you want to be friendly anyway. Ask them how things are going with your work together or something in their personal life. You might catch them off guard and they'll tend to want to keep things happy as a result. Remember: honey draws more bees.

What are some other things that may come up? Your client might ask you for an extension, which you'll be better able to manage on the fly if you're well-prepared, know your overall numbers, and have an idea of how flexible you can be. Again, your goal is to get paid, so are you risking not getting paid at all if you insist on the full amount now versus letting your client pay you over time? It's your call, but think through your options before you head into full-on collections mode.

Getting Paid Strategy: Get Paid – Do the Work

If you're a coach or online consultant, chances are good this is your business model. These days, it's common to set up a marketing funnel, offer a program, and have your clients pay you via an automated system before you even say "hello" to one another. There are certainly pros and cons to this type of set up, but it can be a great way to manage your finances. Getting money up front alleviates the need to track people down to pay you and it helps tremendously with your cash flow. Both are huge pluses for your business.

Let's look at your strategy, planning, and preparation for this payment model. Getting paid up front can take several different roads. Are you expecting 100% payment in advance? Do you have a fixed price for your services, and can your clients pay in stages? Are you working hourly and asking for a retainer up front? Determine what works best for you and your business to set up your process. You may have a variety of options, depending on the mix of services your offer to your clients. For example, I have long-term clients that pay me at the beginning of every month for my financial management and consulting services, and I have financial training clients who pay an upfront fee for multi-week programs. I offer the option to pay all of it right away or the ability to pay in three installments. I rarely do anything else because I've established my payment parameters and stick to them.

Take a few minutes to reflect on your payment strategy. Do you have a defined process – i.e. is it written down anywhere? Think about what meets your clients' needs while working best for your business. When you've developed a game plan in this area, you can simply "set it and forget it" as the money comes in. It can alleviate a lot of anxiety because you won't be recreating the wheel for each new client.

Planning for getting paid up front is fairly easy, too. It's a good idea to identify which platforms will take the payment and deposit it into your business checking account quickly. If you're working online, oftentimes the flow starts with charging your client's credit card. The money is processed by your merchant service provider – PayPal, Stripe, etc. – and is deposited into your cash account a few (or many) days later. Pretty simple. What you need to plan for is how you will stay on top of initiating the process in a timely manner and how you will record the transactions in your accounting system.

The good news with an upfront payment system is that you're getting funds relatively quickly. You're not chasing people down or waiting weeks to get cash in hand. This is a great place to be. The piece you need to be most aware of is determining how you'll use that money. It can be easy to spend it all right away, forgetting to plan for your credit card bill or to put aside money for an estimated tax payment. Spend some time considering how much of each payment you want to set aside for expenses, taxes, and yourself. Doing this work now will help make it a habit when your sales are up and you're busy working with clients.

Turning It Around for a Win

I had a client call me in a panic one day. Michaela had a client who wasn't paying and had basically fallen off the radar.

The client wasn't responding to mailed statements and she was worried she'd either have to take the client to court or write off a lot of money. Michaela thought they had a great working relationship and knew the client was happy with her work, so she was totally surprised she hadn't been paid. She was starting to feel taken advantage of and really didn't like it.

We reviewed the details of the contract, the work she provided, and the timeline together, so Michaela had all the information clear in her mind. Then I told her to pick up the phone and call the client. Michaela *really* didn't want to handle it this way, because she was much more comfortable using email or even texting her clients, but I encouraged her to give it a try. The client answered and Michaela started by asking how she was doing. She told the client she wanted to make sure the client was alright because she hadn't responded to Michaela's latest emails.

There was a pause and, while Michaela waited nervously, the client started explaining that she'd been embarrassed that she couldn't pay Michaela because of some unforeseen medical bills and didn't want to let her down, and, unfortunately, she couldn't cover the invoice right now. See how easy it is to hide from our money? The client was in full-on ostrich mode.

Since Michaela and I had discussed various options already, Michaela felt good offering to set up a payment plan to take care of the balance. The client was ecstatic. She'd been stressed out and hiding her head in the sand, and was relieved to have an avenue to make it right that worked for her. They agreed to a small additional fee to cover the cost of the money and Michaela took the first installment over the phone, with the understanding that she'd charge the same card every month on the same day for the next six months.

The payment plan was a win-win for everyone. Many people are afraid to ask for flexibility and many business owners aren't willing to offer it. Finding a creative way to meet both your needs can be the difference between doing work for free and getting paid what you're worth.

The Cost of Money: Charging Interest and Covering Credit Card Fees

We talked briefly about charging interest on overdue invoices and I want to dive into that a little deeper. Lots of women are conflicted about charging interest. It seems confrontational, doesn't it? Let's drill down on that belief for a second. Do you feel you're *really* worth what you're getting paid? If you answer with a resounding "YES!" then ask yourself this: Is the money you earn of any less value? I mean, if you're worth your fees, then you should be comfortable expecting said fee to hit your pocket in a timely manner, too. Otherwise, you're just giving away your services.

Here's my belief: It's not okay for your clients to treat you like a zero-interest loan. You're not a bank. The money your clients owe you has value. The longer it's not in your hands, the more value it has – in the form of interest. It's a way of taking care of your money and not leaving any on the table. You can write it into your contract and start assessing as soon as your clients have overdue balances.

Another version of this conversation is credit card fees. I know this causes pain for a lot of business owners. We all feel we need to accept credit cards in today's marketplace, but you'd rather not have to lose 2-6% of each transaction to the merchant provider. I feel your pain, I really do. Here's how I look at it, though. Remember when we were talking about how great it is to have money funnel into your account within a day or two of charging your client? That comes with a price. That price is your merchant service fee. So, on one hand, you can look at it through the lens of "nothing is for free" and consider it just another expense. Granted, it's a variable expense because the more you charge, the more you pay in merchant fees, but you get the idea.

On the other hand, that doesn't mean you can't manage it to your advantage. Make sure you're using a provider that works well for your business. You can always check your fees against other options and make changes if you need to. Just because you started with one company doesn't mean you can't swap out for a better deal down the road. Do you have to pay a base rate, which you're charged no matter what, or do you only pay on the transactions you run? The answer to this one question can save you hundreds of dollars a year. You also want to be sure your provider works with all your online platforms before you make the leap. There's nothing worse than spending money only to find your systems don't sync up. If you've been in business for a while, this is probably already set up and running smoothly, but it doesn't hurt to shop around occasionally to make sure you're getting the best deal.

You can also build your merchant costs into your fees. A great way to think about this is to work backwards. Here's an example (caution – numbers coming up): Let's say you offer a monthly service package for $499. You pay 2.6% to your merchant provider (no annual fee), so you end up with $486.03 in your checking account. If you want to have $499 in your account for these services, then you would have to raise your fee to cover the merchant service fee. You could charge $511.97 to meet this goal. Get out your calculator and check the math, if that helps. You may want to consider this and you may not; it depends on how you interact with your clients, the message you want to send, and your own comfort-level. You might just chalk it up as a cost of doing business.

That saying "There's no such thing as a free lunch" is entirely too true. Money in and of itself has value and has costs associated with it. If you can make the most out of what you're earning by charging interest, and make sure that what you're paying for the privilege of playing is reasonable, you'll be in good shape. Make up the difference if you can; you'd be surprised what money you can retain when you strategically plan for covering these types of expenses.

Getting Your Cash Flow On

Okay, we've talked about getting you paid quickly and that's a major part of your *cash flow*. Let's dive in a little further and learn why it's important. You hear people talking a lot about cash flow, but what does it really mean?

Cash flow is simply a way of tracking the money coming in and moving out of your business. In other words, if your cash is increasing, you have positive cash flow. If you have "decreasing liquid assets" (i.e. less cash), you have negative cash flow. It's calculated by taking the amount of money you have at the end of one period and adding in your income and expense transactions that have cleared your bank accounts. If you received more payments than you paid out in expenses in a particular month – thereby increasing the amount of money in your bank account – you have a positive cash flow. It only looks at the money *actually in your bank account*. In the beginning, most of us manage our finances by looking only at cash flow, so hopefully this already makes sense to you.

Your cash flow cycle has a progression. I'm going to use our second payment cycle above as an example. When you agree to do work with your client, you're in a *neutral* cash flow state – no money has changed hands yet. You send a PayPal invoice, which is still *neutral* cash flow. Then your client pays the invoice, and you've got *positive* cash flow when the money hits your account. But don't forget, you still need to do the work, which often includes reimbursable expenses and perhaps paying yourself, so that's a *negative* cash flow stage in the cycle. The cycle starts all over again with the next contract (or an additional work authorization).

Cash flow isn't just about getting money in the door, it's also about how you spend it once it's there. That means keeping an eye on your expenses and managing your bills to your best advantage. It could include reducing your spending or scheduling your credit card payment due date to the time of the month that's most advantageous for you. The bottom line regarding cash flow is this: Your goal is to take in more money than you're spending, so the strength of your business is building.

REFLECTION QUESTIONS

1. How are you getting paid?
2. What's the fastest way to turn your work into cash?
3. What processes do you need to make that happen?

EXERCISE
Receivables

Take a few minutes and think through your payment strategy. It shouldn't take you long to develop a protocol for your receivables (the money you're owed). If you're getting paid up front, how do you track it? If you offer payment terms to your clients, what reminders do you need to set now so you can stay on top of your outstanding invoices? Write down your answers and save them along with your other business documents. That way, if you find yourself getting off track by offering a variety of terms or not following up on past due invoices, you can review your strategy and get back on track. You may also want to write out a call script and practice it a few times. It's amazing how doing this in private can make it much easier when it's time to make the call.

The Take-Away

Whew! We've covered a lot already. By now you're starting to see how establishing a routine with your money can help streamline your business and alleviate some stress. Here's what I'd love for you to take away from this chapter: Establish your payment process and identify problem areas so you can develop the strategy that works best for you. Think about how you might deal with those problems when they arise (because they will). If you make a strategy, plan, and prepare for your business's accounts receivable – whether you get paid up front or invoice your clients – you'll be in great shape managing your income, and you can spend less time making those dreaded calls and more time counting the cash pouring into your accounts.

Chapter 6

Pay the Piper

"We can tell our values by looking at our checkbook stubs."
– Gloria Steinem

How are you feeling? I ask my clients this a lot as we work together, and I want you to feel positive about managing your money. We've talked about getting paid and keeping your clients happy, which is generally an entertaining part of business. This next part is all about the other side of the coin: expenses. A big piece of finding our financial balance is taking a hard look at our spending habits. So many people I work with have a tough time talking about their expenses. They're afraid of being judged. I know how hard it can be to let someone in to look at your financial reality. I hope we can at least get you comfortable looking at it yourself.

The general business community doesn't really help us out. There are hundreds of books and articles, blogs, and social media groups dedicated to connecting with new clients and bringing in more work. This tends to be where people focus their attention. Why? Because increasing your income gives you the most bang for your buck. Want to take home more money? Bring in more clients, do more work, charge higher prices.

It's way more fun to talk about generating income than messing around with receipts, and figuring out our bills doesn't seem sexy. Here's a little secret, though: It *can* be. This used to be my playground. In my previous work, I had little ability to swing the income needle for my company, but I *could* control our expenses by focusing on smart spending, so it's now second nature to me. I found that it can be an interesting puzzle to manage spending without feeling like we were super focused on cutting costs, which can be extremely demoralizing. The staff never knew how much I'd saved over the year, but they sure appreciated the December bonuses. I want this part of your business to be rewarding and feel second nature to you, too.

The trick to making this fun is to look at the bigger picture. If you make more and spend less, that's more that you can put into your own pocket, right? Most people don't enjoy tracking their spending and we tend to find it limiting. We have an emotional reaction to it, like we're a naughty child who expects to be reprimanded by the money police. Here's the thing: *You* are the money police for your business, and you're responsible for your top line *and* your bottom line. If you can put on your fact-finding hat and separate yourself from an emotional response, you'll be able to use your spending habits to your advantage.

So, let's talk a little bit about managing your expenses in a way that's exactly right for you.

Be the Kind of Client You Want to Have

Have you ever had a client blow you off? I'm sure you've had these people in your life at one time or another. Those who take the mantra "Pay yourself first" to an extreme. They're the types that won't pay the electric bill until the third notice is sent, even though they have the money to pay it. I absolutely agree that managing your cash to your best advantage is a good idea because at the end of the day, you have a responsibility to get your needs met. That being said, my biggest rule in business is this: Be the kind of client you would love to have.

Think of it as the Golden Rule for your business. If you want your clients to pay you promptly, then you also need to pay your bills promptly. Want to have great relationships with your clients and have them refer business to you? Work on your relationships with the people who provide services for you and consider how you can help them succeed. It may sound a little *kumbaya* to say it this way, but it's true. Treat others as you want to be treated. It *will* come full circle.

This can come in the form of choosing to buy local for your business instead of online. Maybe you rent an office or use a courier. When you sign up for these services, you're entering a contract, just as your clients do with you. What do you want that relationship to look like? Take a few minutes and think about how you can become consistent in all aspects of your business. How can you create an environment that's in alignment with your goals?

Taking Care of Business: Managing Your Expenses

There are a few different ways you might handle your expenses in your business. They include paying vendors with terms of some kind or putting your purchases on a credit card. You can even barter for goods and services. Let's look at the way most of us work in the online environment.

Quick & Easy: Credit Cards

These days, it's easy to have one business credit card that you use for all your purchases. This may not even be an actual "business" card; it could be a personal one that you dedicate to your business. Regardless of how you do it, as I mentioned in Chapter 3, starting to keep your personal and business spending separate is a good idea.

Since so much of our spending is online, paying by credit card is a simple way to keep most, if not all, of your expenses flowing through one place. I have clients who put everything on a card so they can get points or cash back rewards. This is a great way to handle things for two reasons: 1) you're getting added value through the rewards programs (if you use them!) and 2) you're effectively giving yourself an extra 21-30 days to pay your bills.

You may have already fallen into this pattern without much thought, so let's look at it a little more closely. Again, we want to make conscious choices about our spending, and that includes choosing *how* we spend. When you use credit to pay your bills, there are certainly benefits. You can buy something and not have to pay for it immediately. These days, you can put nearly everything on a card, including insurance payments, utility expenses, even rent. Depending on how much money you have coming in to your business, this may be important... or even critical. If you get paid at a certain time every month, for example, you may find your cash flow fluctuates significantly, so having a few extra days of buffer before paying your expenses can help smooth out those ups and downs.

A word of caution, though: Pay attention to the amount you're spending. If you're not able to pay off your entire balance every month, I'd recommend taking a hard look at your revenue vs. your expenses. I've worked with clients who didn't do the math and failed to realize that by always carrying a balance on their credit cards, they were effectively flushing hundreds (sometimes thousands) of dollars down the drain every year. My goal for you is to maximize the benefit of credit cards and minimize any potential negatives by paying your entire balance every single month. Go ahead and rack up those airline miles and enjoy a free trip to Hawaii! Just try to avoid spending your hard-earned money on finance charges to do it.

A good way to ease into this is by knowing exactly what your spending limit is and working toward paying your card down to zero every month. It may take a while to get there, especially if you've utilized credit to start your business. This is nothing to be ashamed of; many, many people use credit cards this way. Back in the day, you would go to the bank and ask for a startup loan. It's a lot harder to make that happen these days, and credit card companies have stepped into the gap. A good goal is to pay down more every month than you spend so that eventually you can pay it off monthly. If you're in this situation, develop a plan for yourself that includes the date when you want to pay in full. Take a few minutes to review your credit card use and develop a plan for paying down your balance. You can avoid exorbitant finance charges and late fees in this way and start to feel better about your spending to boot.

The great news about living in our online world is that you can easily set up automatic payments of a base amount, the total due in full, or some other amount. You can even pick your due date to coincide with the time of the month when you have ample cash in your checking or savings account. Look at your monthly due date and decide whether you want to move it to minimize the need to add more money from your personal account to cover the bill.

Analyzing Your Spending

Okay, let's get down to brass tacks here. Stick with me, because managing your expenses is one of the most important gifts you can give yourself. I don't mean being a Frugal Jane 100% of the time, or denying yourself trainings, or becoming Scrooge. I'm talking about getting comfortable with your spending so you know *exactly* what you're buying and *why*. I'm a big fan of making conscious choices and your expenses are the perfect place to practice.

When you start a business, it can be overwhelming to see the money pouring out (often long before it starts pouring in). A lot of us go into ostrich mode: I'm going to put it all on a credit card and worry about it later. It's super easy to charge your expenses. You're bombarded with messages about what you *must have* to be successful. You're reading about setting up funnels, and getting toll-free numbers, and building websites. It's simple to slip down the rabbit hole of overspending.

The basic rule of thumb in business, particularly after you've been around for a while, is that you want your income to exceed your expenses. And with this one simple calculation, we're circling around back to the conversation about how much you want to get paid. If you spend all your revenue on expenses in your business, you're not taking anything home for *you*. So how do you stay on top of your expenses? One word: analysis.

I'm sure it's no surprise to you that many of us shy away from reviewing our spending habits, but it's incredibly helpful for your business. Look at your bank statement from last month. What expenses did you have? Were they all necessary? How did they help your business? This is a great exercise to do monthly until you know, give or take a hundred dollars, what you spend each month. Then, once you're on autopilot – with recurring bills, and as many expenses on "set it and forget it" as possible – you can review things quarterly or annually to make any necessary adjustments.

Perhaps you'll realize that you aren't really using that expensive software any longer. Double check your subscriptions and cancel any that aren't moving your business forward. Everyone I know has at least one (most likely more) stories about buying something they thought they *had to have* only to realize after they were up and running that it was a waste of money. That client management system served a need at some point but you're not using it consistently. Does it warrant shelling out $25 a month or can you put that $300 a year to better use?

This is where you can put on your business manager hat and analyze your actual needs against what you're buying. Try to strip out the emotion and don't beat yourself up about past purchases. It won't serve you. Instead try to be wildly curious and use your numbers to answer the questions of where, what, and why. Your reports can tell you the story of your spending and you can use that story to make adjustments that will help you in the long run.

I promise examining your expenses is a worthwhile activity. Too often we get into financial habits that don't serve us, in the same way we get into emotional or physical habits that aren't in our own best interest. You can set a reminder for yourself and just take half an hour occasionally to look at your spending. When you know with absolute certainty that the costs you're incurring are the right ones for your business, you'll be amazed at how confident and secure you'll feel.

Files, Files, Everywhere: Record Management in the 21st Century

Okay, so you're taking care of your expenses. Now what do you do with all those receipts? Maybe you've heard that you need to keep them, but for how long, which records, and how best to manage it all?

If you are like most people, you have a variety of documents related to your bookkeeping and business. This probably includes credit card receipts, bank statements, client payment stubs, and many others. What to do with it all? In today's digital world, many of these documents may come to you in electronic form. Most likely, however, others still arrive via the post office or even fax. All of these documents are important to running your business and they need to be recorded properly and then retained for varying lengths of time. Unfortunately, filing is boring and the last thing most of us (myself included) want to do with our time. Does this sound familiar? You keep throwing receipts on an ever-growing stack at the back of your desk and then wind up chucking it all in the fire a year later? Or worse yet, it sits there gathering dust and staring you in the face every day. Ugh, talk about pressure!

So, what is a busy business owner to do with all this information? How do you manage it and what method do you use to keep it? And most importantly, does that method allow for quick and easy retrieval when you need that one receipt three years from now? Let's review some standard document retention rules and look at a few useful tools you may want to explore to streamline your financial record-keeping system.

Document Retention: Rules of the Road
Your system must be built with the end user in mind: You.

This doesn't mean finding the easiest way to save a file. It's actually about finding the easiest way for future you (or your staff) to *retrieve* a document. If you can't find it, it doesn't exist, right? You want to find a system which makes document retrieval easy and which is simple to understand. Your future self may very well forget where you saved that lunch receipt from 2 years ago, although your current self is certain you will never, ever forget where you stashed it!

You could be spending (or paying for) precious hours searching for that document somewhere down the road. It's a good idea to keep your files simple and easy to retrieve. This can mean filing documents by date, by vendor, by account number, or, ideally, a combination of keywords and data.

What documents are we talking about here?

From a financial standpoint, the IRS outlines exactly what records you need to hold on to. If you follow the rules, you should be sitting pretty if you're ever audited. The IRS has published a handy guide; I encourage you to check it out at www.irs.gov by searching "What kind of records should I keep?" There are a couple of noteworthy items on this list. You'll notice that not only should be you holding on to your credit card statements, you're also supposed to keep the original receipt. It's also important to pay attention to how you record meals, entertainment, and gifts. When in doubt, ask your accountant to clarify what you can expense and what is not tax deductible.

In today's electronic world, most people have a hybrid of paper and electronic records.

What to do? My suggestion is always to move as much to an electronic platform as possible. There's really no longer any need to retain paper copies, (unless they are notarized documents or contracts with ink signatures). Standard day-to-day financial documentation can certainly be kept electronically.

Use a standard file-naming structure that makes retrieval easy.

Seem obvious? The name of the electronic document should tell you right away what it is. You can save tons of time this way, alleviating the need to open and verify documents with names like "July 15, 2016." This will be important for whoever needs to pull the information later on, whether that's you or someone on your team. It's a good idea to make sure your naming system sorts well, so if you're looking by file name you can sort your deposit slips, statements, invoices, etc. together to speed up your search. Again, the goal is to make retrieval quick and easy.

If you do go 100% digital, make sure you dispose of any paper properly after you create a digital copy.

Tossing it in the recycle bin may not be a great idea. Do you have any idea who looks at your trash? I don't either, but I'm guessing you don't need someone at your local transfer station checking out your credit card statement! Shredding is great and you can even compost it later, if you're so inclined. Burning old papers in the fire pit is always a fun option at my house. Marshmallows cooked over old bank statements are pretty tasty, I must say!

There are many ways to set up your system. I recommend spending some time thinking through the documents you generate and receive during the course of your business and taking the time to create a short plan or cheat sheet. Then take some time to put your records into place per that plan. Later, when you hire that assistant you've always dreamed of, you won't have to explain very much – simply hand over your best practices list and you're off!

Welcome to the 21st Century: Useful Record-Keeping Tools

Over the years, I have set up, used, revamped, and screamed in frustration at lots of different record-keeping systems. The one piece of wisdom I've gleaned is this (and we've heard it before): keep it simple. If you are already keeping most documents electronically (in an email folder, for example), good job! That's the first step toward streamlining your life. The next step is to explore ways to help you maintain your records with the least amount of time and effort on your part.

This is where online services can make a huge difference in your life. Whether you're only looking to maintain financial data or want a place to safely keep your contracts and other legal documents, or even a place to share documents with other people, there are a host of options that can seriously enhance your workflow. Do an Internet search for "document retention" and check out your myriad of options. Keep in mind, if you are looking to keep sensitive information such as your firm's financial data in the cloud, be sure that the system you select offers "bank-level security."

Upgrading to Today's Digital World

I have a client who's been in business for nearly 20 years. When we first met, I asked her about her systems to determine whether we could implement any improvements and make her life easier. She was fanatical about keeping her bills and receipts, and had developed a system of tracking her expenses that included a cover sheet for every bill she paid to track which expense account it was entered against. She was *über* on board with keeping her financial records.

For years, she reviewed her bills and credit card statements and wrote out a cover sheet for each one by hand. Then her admin would enter it into her bookkeeping system and process the payment when due. The check stub was attached to the whole packet when paid and everything was thrown in a file. I asked her if she liked the process and she said, "Yes, of course!" Then I asked her how often she had to go looking for a bill in the system. She admitted that whenever she had to retrieve a document, it took a long time because nothing was sorted out, either by vendor or by year. There was no way for her to track anything down.

As part of our work together, I put together a list of recommendations that included moving to an electronic record-keeping system. My client was concerned about moving completely digital, having spent so long pushing paper in her business. I suggested we try out the new system for a month. If she wanted to go back to her old system after 30 days, we could do so and she'd only be out $20 for subscription fees.

Well, that 30 days came and went and my client never looked back. She got over her initial discomfort quickly. She began to see how this new way could save her tons of time on the back end. As a bonus, the program we selected for her integrated seamlessly with her accounting system, so we only had to enter the information once and the expense magically appeared in her finances in the right spot, too. How cool is that?

Later she told me that the biggest benefit moving to electronic record-keeping was the peace of mind it gave her, knowing she could easily find anything she might need later. Her future self was happy, so, despite her initial reservations, she felt great about the new system.

REFLECTION QUESTIONS

1. What does your bill paying look like?
2. What are the areas you can streamline?
3. What's your protocol for keeping your financial records?

EXERCISE
Streamline Your Activities

This exercise will help you clarify how best to manage your business expenses. Here's what I'd like you to do: Review your bank and credit card statements for the past two months and identify where and how much money you spent. List all your purchases for those 8 weeks. You'll start to see a pattern in your expenses. When does your phone bill come due? What about your credit card? How much did you spend on "miscellaneous items" and what exactly were they? Asking yourself these types of questions will help you drill down on what you're spending and analyze whether it's useful for your business. Also, pay attention to the timing. Did you pay anything late? One way to make sure you're paying your bills on time is to review your expenses every week. Enter any bills and check to see if they need to be paid immediately or if you have a grace period. Even taking 10 minutes every Friday to check on your bills can ensure you never pay a late fee again.

The second part of this exercise is to review your activities and record keeping. Are there ways to streamline your work so it doesn't take as much of your time? Developing a plan for your bill paying that mirrors your income flow is a great way to manage your money.

The Take-Away

Managing your expenses is as critical to your success as generating income. Yes, driving your top line – your revenue – is the first place most people look when growing their business, but don't forget to pay attention to your spending as well. This is where the rubber hits the road and by combining solid income with smart expense management your business can really take off.

Hold yourself accountable to your business and be brave enough to really look at your spending. You'll definitely learn something and you may even be pleasantly surprised. If you're a coach or design professional, it's highly possible your expenses can be kept at a bare minimum and you can still enjoy all the tools and training you want, all while putting a healthy profit into your pocket. You may already be in that place, but you won't know if you're rocking the expense side of things until you take a look!

Chapter 7

Timing Really Is Everything

*"Money is the opposite of weather. Nobody talks about it,
but everybody does something about it."*

– Rebecca Johnson

D o you second guess yourself with your finances, wondering *what* to be doing and *when*? I used to feel that way and many of the women I talk with say the same thing about their bookkeeping: "I'm not sure what to do because I don't want to make a mistake." Does that sound familiar? I know for a fact that this paralysis can be excruciating, spinning you down a tunnel of self-doubt and worry. Taking care of your finances becomes a huge weight hanging over you, ready to drop at any moment. It's exhausting, so let's figure out how to free up that energy for something more positive in your life.

The good news is that it's easy enough to overcome those fears. You've already started to let go of those fear demons by reading this far. Establishing a good financial schedule can help you move even further. You'll move from a good entrepreneur to a stellar business person, and from feeling helpless to feeling confident. Even if it feels small, identifying one or two bookkeeping activities and starting to do them regularly can make a huge difference in how you feel about your money management. Whether you're the one doing the work or not, establishing a solid financial routine will help you step into the role of successful business owner. So let's talk about your basic financial activities and how to schedule them into your busy life.

Set Your Money Clock

I tend to be a person who sees things in black and white. (You're shocked, I know.) So, I really recommend getting on track with your money by being systematic about your bookkeeping activities. Certain things need to be done in a certain order and at a certain time. When you're on top of this, your finances will flow effortlessly and you'll be able to spend more time focusing on the things you enjoy. Wouldn't that feel great?

I like to set aside time every week to "take care of business" and it's a habit I encourage you to consider, too. Make it a non-negotiable item on your calendar so you don't fall behind. It's a great way of acknowledging the importance of your financial up-keep. If you make this time sacrosanct – even if it's only 30 minutes to an hour a week – you'll see huge benefits. You won't be stuck facing 10 hours of cleanup and reconciliations to get caught up and you'll have a much better sense of where you stand financially at any given time. Think how liberating that would be!

The general schedule I recommend includes daily, weekly, monthly, quarterly, and annual bookkeeping activities. Some people skip things here or there, developing a plan that works best for them. Regardless of what ultimately becomes *your* protocol, it would be great if the following tasks became a part of your bookkeeping activities. The more often you stay on top of these, the healthier your finances will be.

Consistent On-Time Bookkeeping Pays Dividends

I have clients who are great at staying on top of their bookkeeping tasks and clients who have struggled with the process. For most businesses, (here's that word again) consistent financial practices beat sporadic accounting and reporting hands down. Particularly because it alleviates the stress that comes from not being sure where your money stands. While we can know consistency is important in our heads, putting it into practice is sometimes tricky.

Sasha opened her own marketing consulting business to great success. Right out of the gate, she filled her client roster and found she had more work than she could handle. She was busy with client meetings and getting her branding in place. Money was coming in and she felt she was staying on top of her expenses. Sasha wasn't racking up debt she couldn't pay and she felt comfortable with what she could take home for her personal use.

The one area she had trouble with, though, was staying on top of her finances regularly. She'd let things go for two or three months and then need to spend a whole Saturday getting caught up on her books. She started feeling annoyed and anxious because she felt all these *shoulds* hanging over her head. She was aware that she needed to send invoices more regularly, but couldn't seem to find the time, so emails and statements went out sporadically to limited effect. She was cranky whenever she had to go into her accounting system. Eventually, Sasha had to admit that she needed a better plan for her bookkeeping. She was leaving money on the table and wasn't effectively using her time in this part of her business – and getting irritated to boot.

Getting walloped with a tax penalty because she'd lost track of her payments was the last straw. Being the motivated sort, it didn't take long for Sasha to get herself in order. She made a commitment to her business, developed a bookkeeping schedule that worked for her, and made sure she stuck to it. The next year, Sasha sailed through with increased profit and a confident attitude toward her finances. Her clients responded better to her diligence in financial communications and her reputation continued to grow.

I'd love for you to have similar results.

A Check-In a Day Keeps the Creditors at Bay

I've got a great idea for you: check in on your cash situation daily – at least while you're getting used to this new schedule. It may seem like a lot, but I challenge you to try it for a week or two. With today's technology, it's easy enough to pull up your business checking account on your phone and take a quick peek at your balance.

Do you have a larger-than-normal credit card payment coming up? Or maybe you just upgraded your internet connection and have a one-time charge that you need to keep an eye on. When you check in daily, or at least several times a week, you won't find yourself getting caught short. It's also a fantastic way to get more comfortable looking scientifically at your money situation, and you won't be wondering where you stand with your cash. Take a look at how much money you have on hand and make sure there's enough to cover your commitments.

The Basics: Weekly Tasks to Keep You on Track

Okay, this is where the real work happens, but don't worry – none of it's hard. There are five basic activities to take care of during that 30-60 minutes you've dedicated to your business every week.

Invoice clients: This may seem like a no-brainer, but you'd be surprised how many people don't do this regularly. As we discussed in Chapter 4, sending professional-looking invoices or sales receipts is an important piece of client communication. The timing of it is just as critical. By putting aside time to manage your invoicing every week, you'll generate more consistent cash flow and you'll rarely find yourself overlooking a client or sending the wrong message because it took you three months to send a bill.

Stay on top of your invoicing and I promise you, your business will thrive. Take your weekly time to send invoices or process sales receipts. This way, you won't feel overloaded when month-end comes around and you realize you haven't entered any sales into your system. Looking at it regularly is great for your peace of mind. Even if you only bill clients once a month, I recommend reviewing your invoices weekly, and thinking about staggering your client payment schedules. A great way to manage this is to set up recurring clients for invoicing on different weeks of the month, so you get the bonus of cash coming in more consistently.

Receive payments: During your weekly time, record any payments that have come in. Again, doing this more regularly will help you avoid the end-of-month cringe. It's also a great way to double-check your cash flow. Pay attention to the payments. Did your client pay the last bill but there's still one from two months ago that hasn't been paid? Was there a hiccup with their credit card and you need to resubmit it for payment? The goal here is to simply pay attention to where you stand with your income.

Pay bills: Taking a few minutes to review your expenses should be on your weekly to-do list. Did you buy some new furniture or switch to a new phone company? Even if you don't have bills that are due, double-checking that you have accurate records for purchases and a clear understanding of your expenses is important. You'll find yourself thinking twice before each purchase, which in turn will help your financial wellbeing.

File receipts: One other step in the weekly checklist is to gather and file your receipts and documents. This may include paper receipts from the gas station or finding and saving an Amazon receipt to your files. If you do this weekly, you'll be less likely to skip it later when you have months of records that need to be tracked down and accounted for. You can kiss that March Madness scramble to locate your receipts for the accountant good-bye. How great would that feel?!

Record transactions in your accounting system: All the activities we've already listed need to be entered into your bookkeeping system, too. I list this as a separate task simply to point out that you can generate invoices and review payments in a number of ways, but until that information is recorded in your accounting system, you're not quite complete. If you're set up in an official accounting system, this may be taken care of along the way, but if not, make sure you're tracking your invoices, receipts, bill pay, and expense documentation in your system so you have all your activities in one place.

The Big Event: End-of-Month Accounting Tasks

The good news is that if you're diligent about your weekly bookkeeping tasks, you can easily add in a few more at month-end and be a bookkeeping rock star without too much trouble. Once you get into your weekly habits, it's easy to add on an extra few minutes to do your monthly review. Maybe instead of half an hour, you block out a full hour on the first Friday following the end of the month, for example. You'll be in the financial flow anyway, so this won't be hard to tack on at the end.

Review Accounts Receivable and send statements: If you're keeping an eye on your receivables regularly, this will be an easy add-on. Take a few minutes to review your notes and see if you need to make any calls to shake payments loose. Review your progress monthly and assess finance charges if things are going past due. If you always get paid up front and have no outstanding invoices, cross this off your list and go enjoy the sunshine or a cookie instead.

Reconcile cash accounts: Often when I talk about this, people give me a blank stare. What the heck does this mean, anyway? In a nutshell, it means taking your bank and credit card statements and comparing them to the transactions you have in your accounting system. Do they match up? If they don't, you'll want to make sure you're not missing anything in your books. Most accounting programs include a system for this process.

Review your financial statements: If you're not in the habit of looking at your financial statements, this may be a big add to your bookkeeping task list. Reviewing how much money you made and how much you spent during the month can really help you understand where your business stands. Doing this after you balance your cash accounts is the perfect time. We'll dive into reading your Income Statement and Balance Sheet in the next chapter. For now, try adding it to your list of things to do after the end of every month so it's familiar later on.

Quarterly Tasks: Uncle Sam Wants You (Not to Forget)

Believe it or not, we're getting toward the end of your bookkeeping to-dos! That's the good news. The bad news is quarterly tasks are easy to forget, since they only come four times a year. One little tip that can help is for you to set up a few recurring reminders for yourself. You'll never miss another deadline again and or wake up in a panic, wondering if you've missed something.

Pay your estimated taxes: This task is something we all should be doing. Whether you're a sole proprietor, an LLC, or you file as an S- or C-Corp, you're responsible for paying quarterly estimated income taxes. Depending on your state, you may also be required to file sales tax (sometimes quarterly, sometimes twice a year). Your quarterly tax is definitely an area you don't want to overlook.

"But, Liz," you say, "I don't make much money, why can't I just pay my taxes when I file in April?" It may seem like setting up quarterly prepayments is just adding more to your already-full plate. Here's why it's a good idea to go into the whole quarterlies discussion with your eyes open: penalties. If you miss paying quarterly estimated taxes, you may be on the hook for additional fees. I'd much rather have it set as part of your financial plan and put that money into your pocket. Your accountant can help you determine how much you need to pay and sometimes will even give you pre-addressed envelopes and slips to use.

Another Year Older and in Better Shape

We're so close to the finish line! Once you've established a good bookkeeping routine, your annual tasks shouldn't seem too daunting. I like to start these activities in December, so I'm not scrambling around trying to close out last year while I'm also getting settled into a new one. There's always some level of "living with a foot in each world" at year-end, but starting early can minimize any confusion and keep you from hating your books.

Develop a Budget: December is a great time to work on building your budget. We'll review the basics of budgeting in the next section, so for now simply add it to your checklist to be completed before year-end. You'll want to set aside enough time for this work, as the practice is one that separates the women from the girls in terms of business management.

File Reports and Prep for Accountant: Regardless of whether you do your own taxes or work with an accountant, there are documents and information you need to gather once a year. As a small business owner, you're responsible for reporting your income and paying taxes, as well as filing federal and state reports. For example, if your business paid consultants or vendors who are sole-proprietors or LLCs, you may need to file 1099s, depending on how much you paid them. This reporting is due earlier than your taxes, usually by the end of January.

File Taxes: Once you prepare your tax returns, you need to file them. Your accountant may do this if you have one. If you do your own taxes, whether online or with paper forms, make sure you know all your deadlines.

Record Any Adjustments: So, your accountant may have made some adjustments to your books when putting your taxes together. If she isn't in your bookkeeping system, it falls to you to make updates which you may not record regularly. Not sure what this entails? Ask your accountant and she can walk you through bookkeeping depreciation and other adjustments.

Well done! We just went through a lot of information really quickly. Here's what I'd love for you to remember: Setting up a regular time to keep an eye on your books will make year-end a *lot* easier. If you make a point of staying on top of these accounting activities, you'll be in excellent shape and can face your finances with complete confidence! The key is to start small and get your daily and weekly habits set. When you're regularly looking at your numbers, you'll be more inclined to take care of your monthly tasks, stay on top of your quarterly payments, and feel good heading into year-end and tax season. I want you to know with certainty where you stand and what you need to do next to take care of your books. With consistent attention, your financial garden will bloom, I promise.

Now let's move on to something a little more fun: planning for your future.

Building Your Financial Road Map

Budgeting is a topic that comes up a lot when I first start talking with people about their finances. Usually it's something along the lines of "I know I'm supposed to have a budget, but…." You may even be wondering why I didn't bring up the topic sooner in the book. It's one of those pieces of financial management that's frequently recommended but many of us aren't super clear on how to set or manage a budget. Don't worry, it's one of those things that seems more complicated than it actually is.

I like to say that budgeting is a Google Map for your business. Imagine you took a road trip without your smartphone. I don't know about you, but for me, wandering aimlessly on country back roads without knowing how to get to my destination makes me a little crazy. I'd rather know exactly where I'm headed – and finding out there's coffee shop just up ahead is a nice bonus!

The budgeting process can work in the same way. You know that saying, "If you don't know where you're going… any road will take you there?" If you don't have a budget, you're essentially driving around without a plan or a destination in mind. With a budget, you have a road map for your year. You know exactly where you're starting from and you know where you want to go. The details of the budget describe how you plan to get there.

For a lot of small business owners, budgeting is something that begins a few years in, if at all. It can seem like a waste of time, especially if you feel you're constantly putting out fires as you're working to build your business. The irony is that the budgeting process (like other planning tasks) can help you think strategically and move out of "managing by panic" mode.

So, of course, there are a couple of good reasons to get into the habit of making a yearly budget:

A budget gives you direction. The process of budgeting forces you to take a holistic look at your business and consider what is likely to happen in the next year. How often do you sit down and plan beyond the next day or week? I know if left to my own devices, I wouldn't look much past tomorrow. Taking the time to really forecast your revenue and expenses puts you in a different mindset – a planning frame of mind. The exercise of budgeting allows you to think bigger picture and plan for growth.

A budget gives you a baseline. How do you know when your business is successful? What's your magic revenue figure? A well-built budget can help you identify these important numbers. It may seem like a fruitless exercise to plan the entire next year, knowing that you're unlikely to match the plan. This lack of cohesion can be uncomfortable for any analytical minds out there. If this is you, don't panic.

The beauty of a budget is that it gives you a place to start from. You have your expected income and expense numbers to work from throughout the year. It can be amazingly uplifting to realize that you need to reset your budget because your income is 40% above your estimates. And, it's okay that your actual numbers don't exactly match your budgeted numbers. It's highly unlikely they will ever match perfectly. The important thing is to do the work of building yourself a budget so you have something to compare against. You'll be able to analyze your progress much more coherently.

So how exactly do you build a budget? Nothing could be simpler. You can use historical data from your income and expenses and make realistic projections for next year. List out your income and expenses for the year and divide by 12. That's your monthly budget. Of course, there are nuances to the process, but that's basically it.

I had a client, Marin, who was really freaked out about budgeting. It seemed like a magical, incomprehensible process until we walked through it together. Once we broke down the steps, she started to see how she could set and review her numbers. Now she looks at her budget all the time and feels great knowing she's put a plan in place.

EXERCISE
Your Bookkeeping Habits

A big part of my work with clients includes developing good bookkeeping habits. Everyone goes through various stages when building habits, and this is no exception. It's easy to start off excited, in the "honeymoon phase" when you set yourself goals and are jazzed about learning new skills. Sooner or later, though, that's replaced by the "fight through it" phase. Have you ever gotten really excited about a new diet or exercise program, only to find yourself having a hard time sticking with it past the first few days or weeks? This is the time to put your nose to the grindstone and slog through the process, even when you'd rather ditch it altogether.

With your finances, it's easy to slip back to "I'll get to it later." However, if you can stick with it, you'll eventually move into the "second nature" phase, where you don't even think about the task – it's just part of your normal routine. Or maybe it's part of someone on your team's routine. However it gets done, making it routine is our goal for your financial management.

Now that you have a good sense of how to take better care of your books, take a few minutes and make a plan. What do you want your financial habits to be? How often will you look at your numbers? Where will you go for help? Ask yourself these questions and develop a written action plan and schedule. Then work that plan until it becomes second nature —something you just do. In the long run, your confidence and the health of your business will make it worthwhile!

The Take-Away

We've covered a lot of important information in this chapter. I encourage you to come back to it as you're developing your plan and working on your new financial habits. None of this work comes with a snap of the fingers. Re-read the bookkeeping tasks outlined here and remind yourself that consistency is key. Knowing *what* to do and *when* is a key piece of freeing up your time and your mind from financial overwhelm. Think about all the things you can do, now that worry about your bookkeeping isn't hanging over your head anymore!

Chapter 8

One for the Money, Two for the Show

"What I know about money, I learned the hard way – by having it."

– Margaret Halsey

When I was young, my family lived on a small lake. There was a steep path to our dock where I first learned to swim. As a four-year-old, picking my way down the wooden stairs and peering into the murky abyss was terrifying. To motivate me to jump into the lake, my dad would sing "One for the Money, Two for the Show, Three to Get Ready, and Four to Go!" and we were supposed to leap on "Go."

If you're still with me, you're feeling a lot more fluent in the language of finance and are quickly approaching "Four to Go!" I'm assuming your goal here is to figure out how best to manage your money. You have books that need to be managed, which is why we've talked about facing your financial discomforts and about ways to make non-emotional decisions regarding your business. You've also learned a few new practices for invoicing, getting paid, managing your expenses, and establishing a financial schedule to keep you on track. Hopefully, you're beginning to see how a good financial game plan can help your business grow. Now it's time to talk about selecting an accounting system that works for you, so you can really put your money to its best use.

Pick Your Poison: Finding an Accounting System That's Right for You

I'm guessing this whole topic is the last thing you want to think about. I get that it's not sexy looking at software packages and trying to figure out which one is best for you. But it's an important decision to spend some time on, because you or someone on your team will be using your accounting system day in and day out for the life of your business.

You've heard me use the term "accounting system" throughout this book. A basic definition is "a system used to manage income, expenses, and other financial activities of a business." It might be very simple – a notebook where you record your revenue and costs – or it can be complex – such as industry-specific project management/accounting software.

I know people who have tried five or six different bookkeeping programs before they found the one that fits them best. They might have started out simply keeping an eye on their bank statements, and eventually shifted to tracking everything a little better in a spreadsheet. Some people never move past this stage. I have a friend who's been a successful attorney for the past 15 years and she still manages her finances using the spreadsheet method. She knows her numbers down to the penny and is satisfied with her process as it is. There's nothing wrong with this method *as long as you understand exactly where you stand.*

Most people wind up trying out something more sophisticated at some point. For example, there are various platforms that give you electronic invoicing capabilities and perhaps some expense tracking. They may or may not be part of a project or client management program. Like the spreadsheet method, there's nothing inherently wrong with these kinds of platforms and if you're using one of them, getting paid quickly, and staying on top of your expenses, you may not feel the need for anything more. I would give you one word of caution, however. These programs are often promoted as full accounting systems when they aren't. You don't have your entire financial picture with these types of programs, and you'll most likely need to print out your data and bring it with your receipts to your accountant at tax time.

I've talked with a lot of clients who started their business using one of these kinds of programs and very quickly became aware of their limitations. After learning what they needed to be paying attention to, and realizing that they wanted a more robust system to manage their finances, they moved to true accounting platforms. Generally, they're much happier with their finances because they have all their information in one place. When you can run your financial reports, see exactly where you stand, and learn how to manage your money in a full accounting system, your ability to make smart financial decisions increases exponentially.

You're probably wondering which accounting system I recommend. This book is not intended to sell you on one platform over another. I'm certified in a variety of cloud-based accounting programs and, as far as I'm concerned, you can pick whichever one sings to you. What I'd like to see is for you to seriously consider using a true accounting system that lets you to make adjustments, see your entire financial picture, and gives you statements and other reporting options. Why? So you can set yourself up for growth. Ultimately, you want to be able to pull data from your accounting system that allows you to see how you're doing, compare one period against another, and make sound strategic decisions for your business. But I only want that for you *when the time is right*. If you're happy where you are, keep doing it.

Some of the things to consider when you're looking at accounting systems are:

- Cost (Monthly or one-time software purchase?)
- Number of users (Do you have staff who need access?)
- Fees to upgrade (Are there different tiers and how hard is it to move up?)
- Ability to share data (Can you give access to the system to your bookkeeper and accountant?)
- Accessibility (Can you manage it on the road or with an app?)

- Integration options (Will your other programs work with it to streamline your activities and reduce the time you need to spend entering or re-entering information?)

Having transitioned between financial systems more than once, for more than one business, I can tell you that it's not a process you want to go through regularly. Take your time and talk to the experts (your financial advisors, in particular) before you make your selection. You want a platform that will meet your needs now and well into the future. Will it grow with you and does it have capabilities you may not need today but foresee wanting tomorrow? That's the platform you want.

Why Should You Care?

Alright, by now your eyes may be glazing over and you may be asking yourself whether you really want to find an accounting platform after all. Am I right? Stick with me because next we're going to talk about how well-organized books can help your business soar. We're going to look at the information and reports that show your financial picture.

When you dive into your business's financial world, with a clear understanding of the language and how to use your system, it's easier to identify exactly where you stand. And that's truly empowering. As one of my clients put it, "For years, I'd been meaning to get my finances in better shape, but truthfully, I was worried about not being able to really wrap my head around how it all fits together. And I was scared to really see the numbers in my business. What if this business I've been running with my blood, sweat, tears, and soul was failing? I now understand how my finances work, my books are clean and ready for the accountant, and I know my business is actually successful!"

Now don't think for a second that this client spends all her time messing around in her accounting system. She wouldn't call herself a bookkeeping expert, either. You don't need to be a financial wizard to profit from good bookkeeping. I went into a deep dive in the past few chapters so you can understand how it all works together, but most of us don't become accounting gurus. We leave that to other people and spend our time on things that are more exciting. I encourage you to use this new information to develop a financial strategy that works best for you. And that may include getting help with managing your books.

Whether you do it yourself or hire it out, though, how great would it feel to know for certain that your business was profitable and healthy? It's certainly much better than doing business in the dark, hoping it all works out in the end. To get to this amazing place of financial clarity, you need to get at least a little bit comfortable with the language and financial process. Remember: Doing laundry sucks, but clean clothes are delightful.

Knowing Your Numbers: Your Financial Reports

Okay, how do you put all your financial data into a manageable bundle? There are two main reports that businesses use to review their progress and make strategic decisions. They're called your Balance Sheet and your Income Statement. Don't let the names throw you – they're just templates that show you where your money stands. These reports are built off a series of accounts – known collectively as your Chart of Accounts (or your C.O.A.) – that I like to think of as a series of buckets. You can just call it your List of Buckets (your L.O.B.), if that's easier to remember. Money flows in and out of these buckets as you enter transactions into your system. Your buckets include your assets, liabilities, equity, income, and expense accounts.

Each of these accounts shows up on your financial statements and if you've ever heard someone talk about categorizing or coding their receipts, this is what they mean. When you enter a transaction into your system, it hits one or more of these buckets. The buckets we're usually most familiar with are the expense accounts and these are the ones your accountant most asks about. Think utilities, dues and subscriptions, advertising and marketing. Every time you enter your phone bill, for example, you might tag it to your Telephone/Internet expense account and the amount you spend is tagged to that bucket when you enter it into your system.

The first three types of buckets – assets, liabilities, and equity – are shown on your Balance Sheet, which gives you a point-in-time snapshot of the health of your business. In a nutshell, it shows what you have, what you owe, and what's left over.

The other accounts – your income, cost of sales, and expense accounts – are shown on your Income Statement. You might have heard of this as your Profit & Loss Statement (or P&L) and it's the one that makes the most immediate sense to new business owners. It starts with your income, then subtracts your expenses, and shows what's left over, which is known as your profit. We all tend to think of our money flow this way and it's a great tool for looking at your monthly or yearly progress.

Ideally, it's a good idea to look at both of these reports every month, after you've reconciled your bank and credit card accounts. If you track your numbers in a spreadsheet, you may have already set it up to show your Profit & Loss by tracking your income and expense buckets. Looking at your assets, liabilities, and equity might be new to you, but it's an important perspective, because it's the other half of your financial picture.

I should also point out that these two reports work in tandem. Learning the dynamics of your financial reports is important as your business grows, because they offer insights into what's working well and where you need to make changes to meet your goals. We won't go further into this here, just keep in mind that reading your reports is a big part of knowing your numbers.

Year-End Mayhem

Janet has a wellness coaching business and she spent the first few years simply bringing her receipts to her accountant at year-end and letting him do her taxes. She didn't have an accounting system and she tracked her money via her PayPal account. Because she wasn't making much and needed every penny she earned for her personal expenses, Janet typically drew from her business account as soon as she received payments from her clients and then had to put money back into the business when expenses were due. Since she put everything on a credit card, that meant that she was making transfers several times a week, either out of or into her business account.

There was nothing inherently wrong with this, except that Janet really had no idea how well her business was doing. Things were tight enough that in the back of her mind she thought perhaps things weren't as great as she hoped. The problem was that she just *didn't know*. When her accountant did her taxes, she often had to come up with a chunk of cash that she didn't have. A bunch of her subscriptions were due at year-end so she went into every January feeling like she hadn't made a dime all year.

Janet started working with me in December after she decided it was time to really start understanding her finances. I helped her upgrade to a system that fit her needs and we re-created all her transactions for the year so she could have a clean set of books for tax time. Janet was nervous going into this work because she was afraid of what we'd find. She really had to dig deep and be willing to talk with me about how she ran her business. It wasn't easy for her. Through our work, however, she started to feel more comfortable with the language and to get more excited about the process; she was beginning to understand her finances!

Because we set her up in an accounting system with good reporting, Janet began to see how money was flowing in and out of her business. She could track her business costs more accurately and develop a plan for paying herself that didn't involve making frantic bank transfers every other week. For the first time, she knew exactly how much money she was making and how much profit her business was generating. Janet told me she felt so much better because she had a plan that she could rely on. The feeling of her finances spinning in the wind was gone.

Through that process, Janet completely shifted her financial outlook and year-end is no longer a time of stress and strain. She goes into a new year confident in her numbers and able to focus on her business goals. She learned that while she wants to know how to use her systems, she's not really interested in doing the day-to-day stuff, so she uses her virtual assistant to help keep her transactions entered. She checks in regularly and does the monthly reconciliation and review to make sure everything's still on track. Janet now feels in control of her finances.

REFLECTION QUESTIONS

1. How is my current system serving me?
2. What answers do I need to select my perfect program?
3. What steps will I take to make sure I can track my finances properly?

—— EXERCISE ——
Pick Your Poison

I do this exercise with clients who come to me wondering which accounting system to choose. It's a great way to start thinking about what you want from your program and to start taking charge of your money. Sometimes we slip into a system or platform and we don't really know why we picked it in the first place. Being clear about your needs and goals will help you make the right choice for *your business* instead of just picking whatever passes by in your social media feed.

Look at your financial system now. Does it give you the information you need to make good decisions for your business? How hard is it to export data? Does it generate standard financial reports? Review the criteria I listed above. If your current system gives you all you need, fantastic. Spend some time getting comfortable with how it works. If you can, check your financial statements and notice how money is flowing through your business.

If your current system doesn't meet your needs, it's time to consider other options. See what's out there, ask for guidance from someone who works with financial systems, and find someone to help you move to the new platform. Once you've got a clean system, you can start getting comfortable reading your financial statements and using your data to your best advantage.

The Take-Away

Give yourself a round of applause. Seriously, you just slogged through a *lot* of financial minutiae. I asked you to go all in and you did! Thanks for sticking with me through the financial backbone, reporting, and accounting system conversation. I know it can be rough, but those are important pieces to your financial puzzle. The cool thing is that when you're in a system that runs properly, you don't have to mess around with it much – just pull your reports and review them occasionally. The whole point of this chapter was to help you understand what to look for in a system and where to find your numbers. Now that you have a handle on that, you'll have a better sense of your current system and of ways to find your information so you can run your business better.

Next let's talk about what to do when things go funny, despite your best efforts.

Chapter 9

The Best Laid Plans

"Friends and good manners will carry you where money won't go."

– Margaret Walker

How are you feeling with all this? You may feel like you've fallen down the rabbit hole here. The good news is that you've taken in a lot of new information and are still standing. And here's something else: while I've outlined a financial management approach that will serve you well, there are a million different ways to implement it. So don't worry if you don't know how to read a Balance Sheet yet or you're struggling to sort out how to categorize your expenses. This just takes time to master, but master it you can!

I want you to remember this because even if you follow your plan to the letter, there will be times when the best laid financial plans go awry. You may find yourself struggling to stay on top of entering your expenses or wanting someone to act as a sounding board as you build your business. You may find yourself slipping into "I just don't wanna!" mode, losing track of the positive habits you've been building. So how do we keep your books clean when you really don't want to do the laundry? Let's talk about some problems that may crop up and how to solve them.

The Time Trap: Not Enough Hours in the Day

It can be hard to find time to add all this financial stuff into your life. Sometimes we tack it on as an afterthought and it can be an adjustment to get it in your weekly routine. If the question is "Is it okay that I'm reconciling my accounts at 10 p.m. on Saturday night?" my answer will always be "No!" I'm all about using your finances to find balance in your business – and by extension, your personal time. You need to have a life outside your business, too, after all, and leaving it to the last minute will only make you hate the process more.

I like the idea of scheduling your bookkeeping activities just as you schedule your client meetings or project workload. If you can carve out some time every week to input invoices, pay bills, and look at your cash accounts, you'll be way ahead of the game. You'll start to feel like you're the captain of a tightly run ship.

That being said, you may want to ask yourself whether it's worth your time. A lot of my clients find that even knowing what to do, they're having a hard time fitting the work into their busy schedules. They set aside an hour every Friday morning, only to find they're surfing the web instead. And then there are the concerns about whether you're doing it correctly. Many people find themselves agonizing over generating client invoices or statements, chasing overdue receivables, and getting bills paid on time. Not to mention finding time to balance the cash accounts and review their reports.

If this is the case, it may be time to look for a financial management partner who can perform your monthly activities more efficiently. Someone who has experience, can set you up on automated systems, and offer you financial guidance. If you go this route, you've just gained 4 – 5 hours a month and gained a trusted advisor to boot. Do the math; you may decide it's worth the investment. Think of the prospects you could be meeting, the projects you could be winning, or the clients you could be serving – *every month* – with those extra hours.

The Help Trap: Advisors Who Don't Know *You*

Maybe you've decided you'd like some bookkeeping help after all. "I can use my cousin's wife; she's good (I think) and cheap – what's the big deal?" Here's the thing: you probably have clients who come to you after having listened to their neighbor (or friend or family member) to solve their (business, wellness, marketing, weight-loss, etc.) problem, only to find their issue was made ten times worse. You know that it's important to work with qualified professionals in your industry – why not in your bookkeeping and accounting?

So many people start a business with a passion for helping people and fail to recognize that part of their future success relies on working with professionals who understand their business. Luckily, you now know that there are specialized bookkeeping requirements for your business and that not all financial advisors understand the intricacies of a service-based company.

Partnering with a bookkeeper and/or accountant who specializes in working with coaches and consultants is a great solution. I'd rather see you doing your books yourself or working with trained professionals who know how best to keep your business's finances than picking someone for convenience's sake. While the backbone of a financial system is generally the same for any type of business, there are specific ways to capture the value of your time, and strategies that can help you save money at tax time. Hiring financial professionals with experience working with businesses like yours can make a big difference.

The Delegation Trap: Passing the Buck

It's so tempting. You've got a great VA who could totally take over a lot of this financial work for you. It seems like the simplest, most logical solution to let her do it all. But I've got a question for you. Would you rely on your virtual assistant to manage your retirement funds or determine how to save for your kids' college without your input? So many small businesses rely on their front office staff or VAs to manage their financial systems without much oversight. Now, don't get me wrong. It's not inherently a problem to have others help with your bookkeeping – many administrative professionals are well-trained to manage your receipts and take care of bills, and most are underpaid for the level of service they provide.

But, you work with a professional to help you make other important financial decisions in your life and the same should be true for your other child: your business. Now that you're nearly done with this book, you know how to evaluate the level of financial understanding of your support team, so you'll know which pieces to entrust to their day-to-day care… and which to keep for yourself. You need to have a hand in your financial game and not give it over completely to someone else without serious consideration. As a business owner, it's your responsibility to make good financial choices and your VA simply can't do that for you. And, deep down, you know it's not fair to ask it of her.

Are You DIY?

Once again, it's story time. I want to give you an idea of the realities of small business accounting. I have a friend, Vanessa, who has owned her online coaching business for about five years. She started like many of us do, by paying out of pocket for her startup costs and it took time to establish official business accounts and a bookkeeping system. For the first few years, she really had no idea whether she was making money or not. Since she wasn't taking money out of the new endeavor (she was still working a full-time corporate job), she didn't think it really mattered.

Eventually, Vanessa started getting her financial ducks in a row. She moved to a system that allowed her to invoice her clients more easily and track her expenses. She was feeling like she had a much better handle on where she stood financially.

When Vanessa quit her 9-5 job to focus on her business, she started working with a CPA and she'd simply print out her transaction report and send it along with her receipts to get her taxes filed.

This worked for another couple of years until Vanessa's business was going strong and she wanted to know how she was really doing financially. I started working with her to clean everything up and move her to systems that would integrate with the programs she already had in place. To be honest, she wasn't psyched to spend money on her money, but Vanessa had been in business long enough to realize that she needed to get this right to grow in the way she planned.

Vanessa and I worked together for about 10 weeks. Originally, it was supposed to be 8 weeks, but there was a lot of historic cleanup required, because transactions hadn't been allocated properly for quite a while. The money she was taking out of her business wasn't being tracked so we had to recreate her financial picture.

At the end of our time together, Vanessa had a clean set of books in an online platform that allowed her to work anywhere she wanted and which her CPA could easily access as well. Our training sessions helped her understand what she needed to be doing and we developed a bookkeeping protocol that fit with her schedule. She was feeling great about her finances and I knew she was going to be able to successfully manage her books.

When I checked in with Vanessa a few months later, everything was going smoothly and she was 10% above her budgeted profit. Since she now had numbers to guide her decisions, she knew she had enough to invest in a new training program. Vanessa doesn't need a full-time bookkeeper, but getting help – to establish her system and learn how to manage it – took her business further much faster than she expected.

Getting a Helping Hand

Another client, Deb, brought me in almost from the beginning. She was very concerned about having it done right and was worried she'd make a mistake. Deb is a busy mental health professional, and she just wanted me to take care of it all for her.

I'm not a big fan of taking over someone's books without them understanding what's happening. It's their business, not mine, after all. Deb and I worked together to clean up her accounting system and upgrade her to programs that streamlined her receipt management and bookkeeping. We also implemented a new invoicing process so her patients could pay her more easily, which put money in her pocket faster. Huge win for Deb, who had been struggling to stay on top of her billing and generally feeling like being a small business owner might not be for her.

Now that Deb is set up and running on systems that work for her, I oversee her day-to-day transactions and work as a trusted partner in her business. We make sure to meet monthly after her accounts are reconciled to review her financial reports, and discuss her progress and anything unusual, so she stays in the loop with her numbers. We develop an annual budget and a strategic financial plan for her business, which we track together. This has helped Deb identify areas in her business that were taking too much time and not generating enough income.

She's been able to make some small shifts that have had big revenue increases and she feels better than ever about having her own business.

I share these two examples so you can see how working with someone to get a handle on your finances might help you in the long run. There are lots of ways to get yourself to a point of comfort in your books and that's really all I want for you: to replace fear and discomfort with confidence and control.

REFLECTION QUESTIONS

1. What is my financial cycle?
2. How do I want to deal with my books?
3. Who will I ask for help if I need it?

EXERCISE
Problems and Pitfalls

Whether you decide to go it alone or want to pass off your day-to-day bookkeeping to someone else, knowing how to manage your money will determine whether you're ultimately successful or not. As with anything else in life, the times of strife are the true test of your strength. Thinking about how you might handle a major economic downturn or cash flow problems now will make it much easier to deal with those situations when they come to pass.

Consider these reflection questions: How will you handle problems as they arise in your business? Do you know how to manage your money in lean times? Think about how you might handle difficult situations and write down your ideal outcomes. In a best-case scenario, are you or someone else doing your bookkeeping heavy lifting?

The Take-Away

You can see where things may go awry with your finances. When you're busy or distracted by a new project, it's easy for your finances to go off the rails. It can happen quickly and it can be frustrating to manage, particularly if it becomes something of a habit. You're on track with it all and then you get distracted for a month or two. That puts you back in the stress, worry, fear cycle all over again. I really don't want that for you.

If that's a possibility, given everything you've learned so far, think over how you can get some help. You know where your interests lie, and if taking care of your finances isn't high on the priority list, despite your new knowledge, figure out a way to work with someone who can help keep things rolling. Someone who you can rely on to feed you the information you need to make smart choices for your business. Now that you know what needs to happen, you'll be in much better shape to work with a financial partner, because you're invested in using your numbers to take things to the next level.

Chapter 10

Finding Your Balance

"Money isn't everything, your health is the other ten percent."

– Lillian Day

You know how a skill you've never tried seems supremely difficult and complicated? And once you've learned it, you can't really remember not knowing it or ever thinking it wasn't easy? I used to feel that way about writing a book, and yet here we are. I went from "I could never do that" to "Oh, it's not so hard" pretty darn quickly. Before you started on your journey to financial *Zen*, the idea of feeling supremely comfortable with your money management might have seemed ridiculous to you. I'm hoping that you're feeling further along that spectrum toward "I've got this" after reading and doing the exercises in this book –that you now feel you can look your finances in the face, not with fear but with confidence, accomplishment, and pride.

We've talked about a lot of nitty-gritty financial how-tos together. Hopefully, you've started developing a financial flow that works for you. By now, you've probably seen that in the world of business finance, there are dozens of ways to manage your money. Whatever path you choose will serve you, if it's a conscious choice and not one you've fallen into unconsciously. You now can feel more confident about your income pipeline (contract leads to invoice leads to getting paid) and have come up with a few ways to streamline your expenses. Maybe you've started carving out a bit of time each week for your bookkeeping activities and are seeing the benefits.

Now that you have developed your money management strategy, it's time to talk about planning for your success. My end goal for you is to get to a point where you know exactly how much you can take out of your business to enjoy your life. Now that you have a good idea how to tend your financial garden – or do your financial laundry – you can enjoy all the benefits good management brings, including taking home the bacon. Who doesn't love bacon?

And it's a topic that comes up a lot: How much can I pay myself? How can my business support me? How soon can I take that trip to Costa Rica with my oodles and oodles of cash? (That's my favorite one, too.) It's time to take a step back and look at your overall vision for your business. What do you want out of all your blood, sweat, and tears? Just as there are no dumb questions in my world, there's also no end to the questions you can ask yourself when developing your strategic goals for your business. Enjoy the process, get a little silly, and have fun imagining all the great things you'll do when your business is supporting you the way you dream.

Sustainably Grown Is Financial Sound

Your financial road is going to be curvy. No matter how well we plan, life gets in the way, and it's no different with your business. The unexpected can sidetrack even the best laid plans. So, in the spirit of "expect the unexpected," it's always a good idea to keep a buffer of cash available for those unforeseen circumstances. Maybe you accidentally leave your laptop on the plane or need to come up with an insurance deductible. Maybe you have a personal emergency and you need cash fast. If you can manage your finances with one eye on the future, you've got a much better chance of growing in a steady, sustainable way.

When you start a business, it can be a little like drinking from a fire hydrant. Lots of information is pouring in as you learn how to set up your systems, work with your clients, and figure out how to get paid. Sometimes, we get lost in this state of "turret gunning" and forget to think long term. As far as your financial health goes, putting a plan in place – *in writing* – can go a long way toward maintaining your sanity. I'm sure you've spent some time creating business goals. They might be written down or simply hanging out in your brain, ready when you need them. When you're in the middle of strategic planning, make a habit of looking at your revenue projections and your potential expenses. It'll help down the road when life throws you a curve ball in the form of a new opportunity or a downturn in the economy.

In the long run, this type of forecasting will help keep you grounded as you grow. When money starts coming in fast and furiously, and you're scrambling to keep up with the excitement of new clients and a broader exposure, it's good to have a financial plan in place to help you manage it all. This can go a long way toward alleviating money stress. Because believe it or not, you can feel just as overloaded when you're making lots of money as you can when you're struggling to rub two nickels together!

The good news is that if you can get accustomed to spending even half an hour a week taking care of your books, you'll soon be in the habit of reviewing your finances regularly. It's a small step from there to building a sustainable financial growth plan to guide you through your business ups and downs.

If you haven't seen a great deal of profit in your business yet, that's actually a great place to be. Now that you know how to find out whether you're making money or losing it, take some time to review your current financial standing. Are you seeing consistent monthly revenue? Do you have a handle on your regular expenses? What does the next month or quarter look like for you?

Eventually, you'll reach a point where profits begin to accumulate. The cash in your bank account will start to build up, which is always exciting. There's just one thing I'd like you to remember when this happens: When you start making money, don't start spending it right away.

It can feel so exhilarating to see your cash start to increase and you may have a huge urge to celebrate by buying that new cell phone you've been eyeing or hiring someone to expand your team. I encourage you not to do any of those things right away.

Why? Because building up a cushion of cash is a fantastic way to keep yourself from diving into despair when the economy takes a turn or you have an unexpected expense thrown your way. In every business, there will be unanticipated situations that require a cash infusion, so as you start to make money, keep some of it on hand for a rainy day.

In fact, a lot of entrepreneurs like to have a specific savings or money market account for just this purpose. Maybe it's where you set aside money to pay your quarterly taxes. Or perhaps it's a buffer against a potential insurance claim or the day when you need to invest in your business. If you have a bit of money put away, you'll be better prepared to ride the downturns without stress or worry.

So, if at all possible, don't start spending when you begin to make money – at least not right away or not all of it. And if you're already making a healthy profit, consider putting some of it aside in a rainy-day fund. Your future self will thank you for it, as she lounges without a care beside a pool on a tropical island.

What's Your Reward?

I'm sure you're wondering how it's going to work if you can't spend money when you start making it. You went into business to put some money into your pocket, after all. Trust me, I get the need to earn a living. When can you start taking money out and how do you do it? It can be tough knowing exactly how much is okay to take out and still have a healthy business.

When your business is profitable, there's every reason to assume you'll be able to pay yourself. As long as you're taking care to cover your business expenses and aren't cutting things too close to the bone, you should be able to draw money out of the business for your personal use. This is one of the main reasons we separate our business and personal cash accounts. You can make smart choices when you have a clear sense of what's coming and going in your business.

Ideally, you'll have developed a somewhat regular income stream when you start taking money out of the business. After you've generated a bit of a buffer so you don't have to worry about assessing bank charges for overdrafts or not carrying enough of a balance, there's no reason not to take cash out. After all, that's why you started this all in the first place, right? It's a good rule of thumb to look ahead 45 – 60 days and leave enough in your business checking account to cover any expenses due in the next month or two. If you have loans, make sure you keep cash to cover those payments, as well as any credit card charges you've accrued or expenses you know are coming up. It'll feel so much better to put money in your pocket when you've covered your expenses than to pay yourself first and worry about meeting your upcoming obligations.

Taking this longer view can help in other ways, too. Instead of taking $100 here and $50 there to cover your personal needs, a good goal is to draw cash from your business once or twice a month. Now that you've developed a sense of when money comes in and goes out, you can determine the best times to make those withdrawals. Typically, this is after you've deposited most of your monthly revenue and you've paid off your current debt. It can be pretty liberating to realize you can have a healthy business, and pay yourself twice a month with enough cash to support your lifestyle.

Now, I can hear you saying, "Liz, it's unrealistic to build up cash. I need the money to pay for groceries, my car, utilities...." Here's the thing: You need to do what's best for you. If that means taking out as much as you can as soon as you earn it, so be it. It's important for you to feel in control with your finances. I just know that having a bit of a buffer can alleviate a lot of anxiety about your business, so keep it as a goal, even if you can't do it in the beginning. You can work up to it. Once you're able to establish a balance in your business account, try to keep it topped off so you can avoid those panic moments where you're not sure whether you can meet your obligations.

Sure Things: Death and Taxes

Okay, here's the fun part of the conversation... *eye roll*.... You probably feel pretty negative about the whole tax thing. As an entrepreneur, managing your taxes can be overwhelming in the beginning; there's certainly a learning curve to figuring out the ins and outs that work for your business in particular.

As we discussed in Chapter 2, if you're like a lot of small business owners, it can be a major shift to move out of an employee role into an ownership role. Taxes are a big place to feel this shock. You're used to having taxes taken out of your paycheck regularly and not having to worry about filling out IRS forms or making tax payments because your employer took care of it. As a business owner, you're responsible for it all – that means 100% of federal and state income taxes, and 100% of Social Security and Medicare (known collectively as FICA), so your taxes will probably be higher than you expect. Don't panic.

A good rule of thumb is to put aside 30% to 40% of your profits for taxes. Seem high? It is, by design. It's quite possible your tax rate is closer to 20%, in some cases even lower. The aim is to make sure you're covered and not spending money you don't have. If you put a healthy percentage aside for the tax bill and don't end up needing it all, you're in a far better position than coming up short. You'll avoid that feeling of panic in March when you realize you've earned more than you expected, spent all your cash, and have nothing left to cover your taxes. No matter how much fun you had with those profits, coming up short doesn't feel great come tax time.

It can be easy to think "I'll just deal with the taxes later." Even smart, educated, successful entrepreneurs fall into this trap from time to time. You make a withdrawal from your business for personal use and don't put anything aside to pay for the taxes you owe on that money. You tell yourself you'll make up for it next time. Here's the deal: The bill will always need to be paid, so why not plan for it right out of the gate?

If you create a plan to manage your taxes throughout the year, you'll have easy sailing come tax time. Some people like to stash a portion of every personal withdrawal into a separate savings account that's earmarked for taxes. Others do the mental math to keep the tax amount in their checking account, letting it accrue until needed. Still others squirrel away 20% of their gross revenue every month to fund their quarterly taxes. Whichever method works for you, make the conscious decision to put money aside so you're not caught unaware.

Unfortunately, the government doesn't care whether you planned well or not at all; either way, the bill will be due. For small business owners, our tax payments usually come in the form of quarterly estimated payments and any balance left over when you actually file your taxes. Your accountant can help you establish a baseline that needs to be paid throughout the year, although if there's a big swing from one year to the next, you'll want to make sure you're paying enough throughout the year to cover any increase in revenue.

There are very nice, helpful people at the IRS and it's always okay to call them up and ask questions. In fact, I encourage it. When in doubt, *ask*. This is one of those areas where we all think we're supposed to just know, so we don't want to seem uninformed. Well, we don't always know this stuff and *that's okay*. Think of it this way: If you don't call up your accountant or the lady at the IRS and ask questions, they'll be sitting around their office getting bored. You're doing them a favor by calling up and keeping them on their toes.

The Bottom Line: Paying Yourself

This is the fun part... let's get paid! For most of us, we take it out through what's called an "owner's draw." This may well be how you will pay yourself throughout the life of your business. You can think of it as your version of payroll. Without running a regular payroll with all the reporting involved, you can pay yourself for the work you've put into your business. You take profits out, pay your taxes, and live your life.

Is this the same as payroll? Nope, it's not. A lot of small business owners will talk about paying themselves as payroll. However, that term specifically applies to wages and salaries paid by a company to its employees. As a one-woman shop, this most likely doesn't apply to you, unless your income is high enough and your entity type makes it useful. And if you have others on your team, they may well be independent contractors, not employees, so you pay them a fee, not payroll.

The main reason one-woman businesses don't use payroll, especially in the beginning, is because you don't have consistent income and cash flow to support it. You can't decide one month to have payroll and then cancel it the next month because you don't have enough money. There are strict rules about payroll, so don't go down that road until you're absolutely ready. For the most part, you'll simply take money out of your business via an owner's draw and call it a day.

REFLECTION QUESTIONS

1. How do you plan on paying yourself?
2. Is it sustainable?
3. What's your cash buffer number?

—————— EXERCISE ——————
Run Your Numbers

I have one last exercise for you on this topic of determining what you can pay yourself – a fun one! Let's start by listing out your expected revenue. As you've worked through this book, you've gained the tools to have a good handle on what that number is.

Now list your typically monthly expenses. Again, you should be able to easily list out your regular expenses plus an amount for contingencies. It's a good idea to go low on the income and high on the expense side, so you have a little room for error. There will always be months where your income is down and expenses are up, so plan for it.

Finding your revenue and expenses should be familiar, if you've done the budgeting exercise already. In fact, you can use that information here and the job is half done already! Simply subtract your expenses from your revenue to come up with your profit. Start with your profit number to determine how much money you can take out of the business. Make sure any loan payments are taken into account. Then you can start calculating how much you can pay yourself.

Let's say you're regularly generating $5,000 a month in income. You pay $1,500 toward expenses plus you have a $500 loan payment. Your total cash outlay is $2,000 each month. That leaves you with $3,000 for yourself... sort of. Next, we need to consider how much you want to retain in your business. Remember that conversation about building up a buffer? Perhaps you want to keep $300 in the business for your rainy-day fund.

Now you're down to $2,700 to pay yourself. Sounds okay, except let's not forget about your taxes. Like I said, some people keep money for taxes in their business account and others transfer it out. For this example, if you set aside 40% for taxes, you'll want to keep an additional $1,080 in your account for taxes, leaving you with $1,620 to transfer to your personal account to live on. Alternatively, you might transfer the full $2,700 and put the $1,080 into a separate savings account, still leaving you $1,620 for your own use.

You begin to see pretty quickly that making $5,000 doesn't mean you take home anywhere near that amount. By way of comparison, that's equivalent to $405 in weekly take-home pay from a traditional job. There are two points to this exercise. First, it's important to really know your numbers; when you do, you can determine how much you can pay yourself without getting caught short. When you run your numbers consistently in this way, you'll have an excellent understanding of just how much you can pay yourself – and you can always adjust as you grow.

The second purpose of this exercise is to remind you to keep an eye on your expenses and income. A small shift here and there can have a big impact on your bottom line. If you're able to adjust your revenue even a few hundred dollars a month and find areas to reduce your expenses by another couple of hundred in our example above, you could find yourself taking home $2,000 a month instead of $1620. As a friend and business coach once told me, "Small hinges swing big doors." By paying attention to these incremental ins and outs of your business, you'll be in a fantastic position to build the future of your dreams.

FINAL REFLECTION QUESTIONS

1. What are the three most important things you learned?
2. How will you implement financial best practices?
3. Where do you envision your business going now that you know how to manage your finances?

Speaking of Your Dreams...

I'm so excited for you! You've taken on a super tough area of your business here. I hope you can put this learning to good use and build something you're proud of: A business that you love that loves you back, with great profits and endless possibilities. By now, your personal financial vision is clearer (and rosier) than it was when you started reading this book. It can be amazingly grounding to establish a solid financial foundation. As a client said recently, "Sometimes I get into [my financial system] and just enjoy looking at the numbers. It feels so good to see it and know what it all means. I never would have guessed that would excite me!"

My greatest wish for you is that your business is a huge hit. That sooner rather than later you'll find yourself needing to hire someone to help you take care of your books because you're just so darn busy being stupendously successful. Now that you know how your business's finances work, you're that much more capable of taking things to the next level and growing your business with confidence.

And I also know that pieces of your financial puzzle may not fit everything we've talked about here. Take what you need and find useful, and leave the rest. Anything you do to get better acquainted with the inner workings of your finances is great, as far as I'm concerned. In the end, I just want you to feel comfortable and confident in your business. If anything in this book helped you move in that direction, we've accomplished a lot. So, pat yourself on the back and feel good that you're moving toward total alignment in your business outlook.

The Climb Was Tough. Now What?

You've learned how to do your financial laundry (no, *not* money laundering). You've absorbed a lot of new information, stuff you may instinctively shy away from. If you only take away one thing from this book, I hope it's this: Money management might not be your favorite topic, but it doesn't have to be stressful. There's a clarity to be found in financial consistency. Your business can thrive when you know exactly where you stand.

When you know your money situation, you can make smart decisions with the peace of mind of knowing that you're not missing anything critical to your success. So, as you put this new knowledge into practice, please keep that in mind. Money in and of itself is just a tool. It's not bad, it's not good... it just is. As you shift from viewing money through an emotional lens and start looking at your numbers without fear, you'll reap tremendous benefits. Your business will prosper and, by extension, so will you.

That's easy to say, I know. And maybe you're wondering exactly what next steps to take. Here are a few of your options:

1. Do nothing. Take all this information and leave it hidden away in your brain, put the book on a shelf. At some point, you'll need it, and you can pick up where you left off, or go back and peek at some of the how-tos as questions come up. The info will still be here for you.

2. Take what you've learned here and apply it to your business. Download the *Zen Calculator* and start finding your financial balance. Be a rock star with your money just as you are in every other area of your life!

3. Work with me to get everything squeaky clean, choose platforms that will grow with you and your business, and let me help you develop a financial plan that works for you. Take advantage of my expertise to get your books in order so you can focus on doing what you love, knowing I've got your back. You can get started by visiting www.coachescfo.com/partner-with-me. Can't wait to hear from you.

Share Your Success

I've got good news! It turns out talking about money doesn't have to be taboo, especially when bringing it into the light of day can help you become as confident in your money management as you are in other areas of your business. As an accomplished, passionate entrepreneur, you now have all the tools you need to be great at one more thing: Taking care of your books.

I'd love to hear about your financial progress and I know that others can learn from your experiences, too. If you're finding some time for your finances and starting to see results, share your story! Visit www.coachescfo.com/stories and tell us about it.

Thank you for joining me on this journey. I wish you a great bottom line in all you do.

Further Reading

Sacred Success by Barbara Stanny – An important read for any woman struggling to come to terms with her money and the emotional responses that can keep you from finding true, heartfelt success.

The Feel Rich Project by Michael Kay – A wonderful introduction to personal financial management, with a focus on money mindset while developing a plan for your future.

The Entrepreneur's Garden by Divya Parekh – This book does a beautiful job holding the reader's hand through the process of identifying your important relationships as an entrepreneur.

Your Million Dollar Dream by Tamara Monosoff – A great book to help you identify what you really want out of your business and how to take the entrepreneurial leap with confidence.

Beyond the E-Myth by Michael Gerber – A perfect addition to the E-Myth series that shows you how to create the business of your dreams on your terms.

Acknowledgments

For a long time, the idea for this book was percolating in the back of my mind. It's here in your hands thanks to serendipity and opportunity, covered with a bushel of helping hands.

First, thank you to all the smart, creative clients I've had (and will have) the pleasure of working with. They are at the core of this book. They've helped me craft my practice with their invaluable feedback and endless kindness as I've learned from my mistakes. They've taught me far more than I've taught them. Their willingness to face their financial discomforts and bring their A game to their businesses is inspiring. They're taking things to the next level in major ways and it's a joy to see.

Big thanks to M. and E., for setting me on my own entrepreneurial path. Without them walking with me through the baby steps of my business and reading draft copy, I wouldn't have been able to take *myself* to the next level.

Of course, thank you to the incomparable Angela Lauria, Grace Kerina, Anna Paradox, and the rest of the fabulous staff at Difference Press without whom this book would still be a thought bumping around in the back of my brain. It's been a journey I didn't expect, and one I'll never forget.

To the Morgan James Publishing team: Special thanks to David Hancock, CEO & Founder for believing in me and my message. To my Author Relations Manager, Gayle West, thanks for making the process seamless and easy. Many more thanks to everyone else, but especially Jim Howard, Bethany Marshall, and Nickcole Watkins.

There's an entire community of fellow-authors who walked this road with me and who I proudly call my friends. Their generosity and kinship have been life-changing.

To my beautiful family, a ginormous thank you for sticking by me as I lived in my head during this process. I'm forever grateful for their love and support, as well as insisting on reminding me there's a life outside of work, no matter how hard I tried to forget it.

Thanks to my dad, who taught me the thrill of new ideas and how to dive into them; and for my mom, who showed me the joy of helping others.

And lastly, a heartfelt thank you to *you*, my readers. This book was written in the hope that you find a balance in your books and your business that allows you to live life on your own terms. I wish you wealth and prosperity, however you choose to define it!

About the Author

Liz Lajoie helps motivated coaches and creative professionals master their finances so they can grow an amazing business with confidence. She teaches new and not-so-new entrepreneurs how to set up and take care of their books so they can get the most out of their money. Working with clients throughout the US and Canada, Liz specializes in financial  management and strategic decision-making, helping her clients focus on doing what they love as they grow. She understands how hard it can be to juggle the demands of entrepreneurship and knows having someone in your financial corner can make all the difference.

She helps her clients let go of their financial fears, establish good money management practices, and become confident in their strategic decisions. She loves supporting them as they learn the ins and outs of smart financial management, helping find ways to increase profits while decreasing stress associated with this part of their business.

Liz has spent over 15 years in small business management, honing her skills in finance and bookkeeping for professionals who "sell their brain" for a living. Along the way, she earned an MBA and learned exactly what it takes to run a successful small business. Liz's passion is helping her clients have the business of their dreams, secure in the knowledge that it's built on a strong financial foundation. She lives with her family in northern New Hampshire.

Website: www.coachescfo.com

Email: partner@coachescfo.com

Facebook: www.facebook.com/coachescfo

LinkedIn: www.linkedin/in/lizlajoie

Thank You

Yay! You've dragged yourself through all the uncomfortable new money language and faced your financial discomforts to get here. Hopefully, you're feeling invigorated and confident about your finances and you're ready to approach your business with new eyes.

To help you take your efforts to the next level, I created your *Zen Calculator*, a great tool to help you get started on the right foot. It reveals your top money-making numbers to help you analyze where you stand today and define where you want to go. It's a little bit of financial love and support from me to you. It'll help you develop *your* plans in a way that works best for *your business* so you can grow the business of your dreams!

You can download the calculator at:

www.coachescfo.com/zencalculator

It's a superb way to jumpstart your financial momentum and stay on track with your money management.

Morgan James
Speakers Group

www.TheMorganJamesSpeakersGroup.com

We connect Morgan James published authors with live and online events and audiences who will benefit from their expertise.

Printed in the USA
CPSIA information can be obtained
at www.ICGtesting.com
JSHW082340140824
68134JS00020B/1788

9 781683 507048